D1593493

INTERPRETING
THOMAS MORE'S
UTOPIA

. . . I cannot agree with all that he said. But I readily admit that there are very many features in the Utopian commonwealth which it is easier for me to wish for in our countries than to have any hope of seeing realized.

Thomas More's
concluding words
in *Utopia*

VTOPIAE INSVLAE FIGVRA

INTERPRETING
THOMAS MORE'S
UTOPIA

Edited by
John C. Olin

Fordham University Press
New York
1989

TO MY SON THOMAS
AND MY TWO GRANDSONS
WHO ALSO BEAR THAT
HONORED NAME

Contents

Editor's Preface

On October 17, 1985, we held a symposium at Fordham University on Thomas More's *Utopia* to commemorate the 450th anniversary of More's death and the fiftieth anniversary of his canonization. This volume presents the papers developed from that occasion as well as the remarks by Mario M. Cuomo that opened the symposium. A concluding essay on "The Idea of Utopia" is appended. More's famous book has been called an open-ended dialogue, and we thought that there was no better way to mark these important anniversaries we wished to commemorate than to continue the discussion More began long ago. It is a discussion, we might note, that is seemingly inexhaustible, so many and so provocative are the issues More raised and so varied the interpretations and points of view his classic has inspired. Thus we seized the opportunity to add our contribution to the ever-continuing debate.

Having frequently read in the press that New York's Governor Cuomo had high regard for Thomas More, whom he often quotes and whose picture hangs on his office wall, we took the initiative of inviting him to speak at our conference. We were delighted and not a little surprised when in mid-summer he informed us that he accepted our invitation. He said he wished to make some introductory remarks at the gathering we planned. Arriving by helicopter on the Rose Hill campus the afternoon of the symposium, Governor Cuomo delivered the memorable comments we publish here. They are a moving testimony of his devotion and his debt to the great English lawyer, statesman, and saint. He makes a reference to *Utopia* to which I should like to call particular attention. Linking More with Teilhard de Chardin, Governor Cuomo stresses that the contribution of both men by virtue of their Christian humanism was to reconcile God and the world. The author of *Utopia,* he tells us, sought "to Christify matter," to bring earth to perfection. It is a lesson the Governor has taken to heart.

The other three speakers we invited were obvious choices. Each one is a More scholar well acquainted with *Utopia* and its author.

Their essays give ample evidence of the variety of approach and interpretation More's book can produce. I shall briefly introduce them here and say a few words about the theme each develops.

George M. Logan is Head of the Department of English at Queen's University, Kingston, Ontario, Canada. He is the author of *The Meaning of More's* UTOPIA (Princeton University Press, 1983) and of various articles on Renaissance literature and Renaissance humanism. He is co-editor of the *Norton Anthology of English Literature* (5th edition, 1986) and with Robert M. Adams of a new critical edition of *Utopia* which will appear in the Cambridge Texts in the History of Political Thought series. We asked him to give a broad introduction to *Utopia* at the symposium.

Professor Logan's essay is a penetrating analysis entitled "The Argument of *Utopia*." He interprets the work as a rhetorical exercise examining and testing the relationship of the moral and the expedient in the political realm, and he analyzes both the discussion in Book I of *Utopia* and the "best-commonwealth" narrative in Book II in that light. It is an unusual approach to More's book, though it is derived from classical rhetoric and is certainly in keeping with the Renaissance humanism of More and his contemporaries. That it is a rewarding theme to pursue in deciphering this "deeply enigmatic book," as Professor Logan calls it, is clear.

Thomas I. White is a member of the faculty at Rider College, Lawrenceville, New Jersey, and the author of two notable articles on our subject: "Aristotle and *Utopia*," *Renaissance Quarterly* (Winter 1976), and "Pride and the Public Good: Thomas More's Use of Plato in *Utopia*," *Journal of the History of Philosophy* (October 1982). His topic at the symposium was "Pride and *Utopia*: The Arrogance of Wealth and Power," a subject whose contemporary relevance he stressed. His essay here is a revision of his original theme.

Professor White's essay, entitled "The Key to Nowhere: Pride and *Utopia*," interprets More's book in terms of the sin of Pride, the source of all social evil. It is the central theme in both Books, as he views it, and bridges the gap between opposing interpretations of the work—in particular between George Logan's and Richard Marius'. His discussion here provides an interesting supplement to the previous essay.

Germain Marc'hadour is Professor Emeritus of English literature

xii

at the Université Catholique de l'Ouest in Angers, France, and a founder of the international Amici Thomae Mori and director of its quarterly journal, *Moreana*. He is indeed the dynamic *animateur* of that association and has traveled and lectured widely to promote the study of More as well as a more personal devotion to him. He is the author of many books and articles on the scholar and saint and has been a long-time collaborator in the Yale edition of The Complete Works of St. Thomas More.

Abbé Marc'hadour's essay, entitled "*Utopia* and Martyrdom," tackles "a most implausible theme," as he admits, and is somewhat different from the conventional discourse on *Utopia*. It is a reflection on the notion of martyrdom—that is, Christian witness and heroic sacrifice—in the context of More's famous book. Essentially, Abbé Marc'hadour contrasts Christian spirituality in this regard with the asceticism of the "religious par excellence" among the Utopians, a group known as the *Buthrescae*.

I have written an essay exploring the general idea of utopia and have added it to the others in this volume. I felt such an inquiry would complement the papers of the symposium and give background and perspective to their more specific themes. My essay is an historic *aperçu* extending from antiquity to our own times. It is interpretive and, I hope, suggestive of the broader dimensions and deeper aspects of the utopian vision.

I want to thank my son John and my son-in-law Tony Santos as well as my good friend George Peck and a visitor from mainland China, Qihong Shi, who was a perceptive witness of the Communist revolution in his native China, for their comments and critique. Their discussions with me on the broad topic of utopia have been of great profit.

Fordham University   JOHN C. OLIN
June 22, 1989   Professor Emeritus

1

A Personal Appreciation

Mario M. Cuomo
Governor
The State of New York

It was a privilege for me to receive the invitation to make some small contribution to this symposium. Let me begin that effort with a personal anecdote.

Many times over the years, I have had a visitor enter my office and quickly focus on the print of the swarthy, intent European gentleman in dark, richly-colored robes, chancellor's chain, and peculiar hat who shares my workspace. And more than once, one of these visitors has remarked that I must be very proud of my Italian heritage to have a portrait of Christopher Columbus in such a prominent place on my office wall.

"I am very proud," I say. But unless I have a lot of time, I do not tell the long story of my association with the man in the portrait. I just nod and think how he might have enjoyed the moment, because there never was a man more ready to laugh—especially at his own expense—than Thomas More. That is, I guess, *part* of the reason for my devotion to this complex man whose access to sainthood was, in the end, such a frighteningly simple affair. Thomas More reminds me to take the world, and myself, less seriously.

If that were the whole of his imprint on my life, I should be very grateful indeed. But it is not; far from it.

Thomas More has made the difficult work of fashioning a Christian life more understandable for me, though his own life—and especially its spectacular culmination—has made emulation a hard challenge, to be sure.

He probably enjoys knowing that the story of his life is full of paradoxes and wryness. It is one of the reasons that his story is such a useful instruction to so many of us in so many ways. I have always enjoyed knowing him, and continue today the struggle of learning from him.

I first met Thomas More when I was a young lawyer, and he already an established one. For a while, like others, I cast about for something more than I could find among the conventional wisdoms that were freely dispensed in the courthouse corridors of Kings and Queens Counties, something more than how to make your own breaks, and a buck, plying the craft and trade of a lawyer. I can still remember my excitement at the realization that the facts and unconventional wisdoms of More's life might create new possibilities for my own. Back then—and maybe even today—it was not the scholar or martyr or statesman I was interested in so much as the man of palpable ambition who had managed to set a course that included rising in the world, raising a family, and living as a Christian—and doing all three extremely well.

My sense of morality at that time was still under the sway of the Scholastics. Staying on the side of the angels seemed—at least for someone who grew up in St. Monica's parish, South Jamaica, Queens, fifty years ago—to depend as much on scrupulously applied spiritual accounting principles as on the sacraments. It was a condition that someone in love with the rigorous order and discipline of the law found comfortable enough.

Thomas More was a moralist, and I could use him as a spiritual umpire telling me whether some action or ambition I had stumbled into or contrived was fair or foul. But he eventually did much more for me. He taught me a new subtlety. He had loved God *and* the world, which in those days still seemed an unlikely balancing act.

Thomas More and his world still seemed remote from mine at that time, though. And, as I reflect on it, I think admiring him may have been easier from that distance. When the Second Vatican Council unshuttered my own Scholastic inclinations, I found, along with a fuller, freer sense of my religion, a growing appreciation of More and the subtlety he demonstrated. He was not someone who had gained heaven by spending his time resisting a close connection with the world, seeing it mostly as a series of moral obstacles. I came to realize that *he* had done what the Council was now telling *all* the faithful they must do: love God, not by turning away from the world, but by actively and creatively engaging it. Love Him in His work.

Then came the holy scientist and genius-poet to lend still another dimension. Teilhard de Chardin, in his new articulation of Christian humanism, helped me to see how Thomas More could have appealed as much to the sensibilities of the pre–Vatican II as to the post–Vatican II Church. "Any man truly devoted to the human," Teilhard had written, "must be possessed of great detachment if he is to immerse himself in the concerns of the earth."

It was Thomas More's detachment, his Platonic side, if you will, that had attracted me at first. And then, after the Council, after Teilhard, it was his passionate concern for the world, his Aristotelian side, that caught my, and the rest of the world's, attention. Thomas More was able to reconcile these apparent opposites within his life. He was both man of action *and* Christian mystic. What a nice and convenient combination. For me—still struggling, terribly limited—his life represented a kind of ultimate reasonableness.

Teilhard offered confirmation. "To be fully human and fully alive," Teilhard wrote, "a man must first be centered on himself, then centered away from himself in others, and finally centered beyond himself in Someone greater than he."

Wasn't that precisely the spiritual progress of Thomas More's life? Wasn't his great capacity for life founded precisely on his detachment from the vanities that clutter up the rest of our minds? And wasn't his great death founded precisely on his deep awareness of Someone greater than he?

Whatever the answer, I know my own progress into public life was made at least more comfortable, if not any easier, by the example of Thomas More, and the exegesis of Teilhard.

Teilhard said of his own mission that it was "to reach heaven by bringing earth to perfection. To Christify matter." "To Christify matter." What a startling phrase! What a startling idea!

Is there anyone whose name has been more closely linked to the task of bringing earth to perfection than the author of *Utopia*? That is exactly the enterprise that Thomas More threw his whole life into. For myself, I feel, in a very real way, twice blessed that I can look to this man not only when I am wondering over what I am supposed to be, but also when I am worrying over what the role of government is supposed to be.

In Thomas More's vision of the just society, the wealth of the nation did not trickle down, the way it did in Tudor

England, if you can imagine such a ruthless system. Rather, it was shared, with the spirit of a family sitting down to table together.

In fact, Thomas More based his whole wonderfully detailed program for the reform of society on the same principles with which he ran his own household: the idea of family. It was an idea that was too simple to suit the cynics of Thomas More's time, just as it is too simple to suit the cynics of our own time. But if Thomas More's life teaches us anything, it is that the truth, for all the subtlety and complexity that may surround it, is finally a simple thing, as simple as his solitary refusal to take an oath that would place his soul in jeopardy—even though he might appear, for all the world, as great a fool as the God–Man he followed.

"The road to heaven is the same length from all directions," Raphael Hythloday observes at the beginning of *Utopia*. I think most of us would like to believe that saints travel a shorter road. Thomas More's splendid, eventful life is a reminder they do not.

Let me confide to you that in the last few years I have come to a much greater appreciation of the kinds of temptations that Thomas More must have contended with. And let me confess that I have more need of his counsel now than I ever imagined I would when I first turned to him. My debt to him grows.

I should like to close by commending Thomas More not just as one of history's truly great men, or as an eminently suitable subject for political or literary analysis, but in the way I feel best qualified to commend him—as a companion of unlimited generosity and unparalleled good grace.

2

The Argument of *Utopia*

George M. Logan
Queen's University

Utopia IS A DEEPLY ENIGMATIC BOOK.[1] To be sure, its *subject* is clearly indicated by its full title: *de optimo reipublicae statu deque noua insula Utopia*—"Concerning the Best Condition of the Commonwealth and the New Island of Utopia." This title identifies More's book as belonging to the oldest genre of political writing, the discourse on the ideal commonwealth initiated by Plato's *Republic*. But if the subject of the book is clear, its *argument* on that subject is not. In the first place, after a prefatory letter to More's friend Peter Giles and a few pages introducing Raphael Hythloday, the fictitious voyager to Utopia, the book enters not on a discussion of the ideal commonwealth but on a long debate on whether it is worthwhile for an intellectual to enter practical politics by joining a king's council. Hythloday says "No"; More and Giles say "Yes." Within this debate is another, recounted by Hythloday, on the problem of theft in More's England. And when, at the beginning of Book II, we at last reach Hythloday's account of the new island, it is by no means clear exactly what the relation is between that account and the topic of the best condition of the commonwealth. As R. S. Sylvester points out, the ambiguity of this relation is hinted at in the title itself: "concerning the best condition of the commonwealth *and* the new island of Utopia."[2] Is the new island (as most readers over the centuries have thought—hence the meaning that More's coinage "Utopia" has taken as a common noun) an embodiment of what More takes to be the best condition of the commonwealth, or is it rather (as a number of more recent readers have thought) a counter-example, an example of what More thinks a commonwealth ought *not* to be? And then there is the third possibility, which is preferred by still others (by most people nowadays, I would guess): that Utopia is partly More's ideal, and partly not.

This view has in fact much to recommend it. The commonwealth of Utopia is highly attractive in some ways, and highly unattractive in others. No one goes hungry there; no one is homeless. The commonwealth is strikingly egalitarian. On the other hand, personal freedom is restricted in ways large and small. Discussing political issues outside the senate or the popular assembly is a capital offense; a citizen must get permission from the local magistrates to go on a vacation, and from spouse and father even to go for a walk in the country. In general, if Utopia anticipates the welfare democracies of our own time in many respects, the elaborate constraints imposed on its citizens also frequently put us in mind of modern totalitarian regimes. More's own society was rigidly hierarchical and highly regulated, so Utopia may not have seemed as restrictive to him as it does to us. Still it is difficult to believe that he would have regarded as ideal all the features of Utopia that we find unattractive. But if his imaginary commonwealth mixed features that he thought ideal with others that he did not, why did he make it so? It is easy to understand why a writer would want to depict an ideal commonwealth or to satirize a bad one. But why would anyone undertake to invent a commonwealth that is partly good and partly bad? A writer with that end in view would scarcely need to resort to fiction. And if Utopia is a mixture of things More thought ideal with things he thought un-attractive, what is the principle of the mix? How did he determine which parts to make ideal and which parts not to? Or is Utopia simply a whimsical mélange? And, finally, what exactly do the debates of Book I have to do with the account of Utopia in Book II, and with the subject of the best condition of the commonwealth?

This last question offers a good starting point, both be-cause it starts us appropriately at the beginning of the book and because it is not hard to find some answers to it. Thus it is clear that one thing that the debates about Europe in Book I have to do with the account of Utopia lies in the fact that the juxtaposition of the two throws into relief what is wrong with Europe and what is right with Utopia. This is the burden of the peroration of the book, in which Hyth-loday eloquently sums up what it has shown us both about Europe and about Utopia, and makes, very powerfully, the comparisons that are begging to be made. In Europe, he says, accurately summarizing what we have seen in Book I, "men talk freely of the public welfare—but look after their private interests only" (239/1–2).[3] In Utopia, by contrast, "where nothing is private, they seriously concern them-selves with public affairs" (239/2–3). And who would "be so bold as to compare" Utopian justice "with the so-called justice prevalent in other nations, among which, upon my soul, I cannot discover the slightest trace of justice and fairness" (239/26–29)? Having read Hythloday's excoriating analysis of English and European "justice" toward the poor, we can hardly fail to agree, as we must also with his summary statement that "when I consider and turn over in my mind the state of all commonwealths flourishing anywhere today, so help me God, I can see nothing else than a kind of conspiracy of the rich, who are aiming at their own interests under the name and title of the commonwealth" (241/24–29). Of course Hythloday—who is the prototype and patron of all those who have thought Utopia an ideal commonwealth—fails to mention a few respects in which the juxtaposition of Europe and Utopia throws into relief shortcomings in the *latter.* But when, for example, we have encountered in Book I Hythloday's scathing condemnation of the use of mercenaries (which he associates especially with the dastardly French), it is impossible to read with entire equanimity that the Utopians are major employers of mercenaries. Similarly, since Hythloday argues so memorably that "he who cannot reform the lives of citizens in any other way than by depriving them of the good things of life must admit that he does not know how to rule free men" (97/2–4), we are likely to use this sentiment as a standard by which to evaluate the repressive life of Utopia. Moreover, such comparisons, whichever way they happen to cut, are also clearly relevant to the topic of the best condition of the commonwealth. In particular, the analysis of European problems—the reminder of just how far Europe is from the best condition of the commonwealth—both provides the appropriate context for musings on the ideal commonwealth and adds urgency to them.

Book I also contributes to the discussion of the improvement of commonwealths by illustrating a powerful method for the analysis of social problems and the formulation of solutions to them. In the debate on theft in England, which Hythloday says took place at the table of John Cardinal Morton, Henry VII's chief adviser, Hythloday argues with an English lawyer who purports to be amazed that the country remains infested with thieves, seeing that "so few . . . [escape] execution," with "as many as twenty at a time being hanged on one gallows" (61/12–14). This lawyer has a rather shallow understanding of the problem of theft: he takes it for granted that its cause lies in the wickedness of thieves, and that its solution therefore lies in capital punishment, which eliminates actual thieves and should deter potential ones. By contrast, Hythloday finds the immediate cause of most theft in poverty, which places many Englishmen under the *"necessity* . . . of stealing" (61/29; emphasis added). In turn, poverty is the product of a number of social factors: wars, the existence of idle, parasitic classes, and the spread downward through the social scale of the luxurious tastes of the upper classes. Thus Hythloday finds the root causes of theft not in the bad character of individual thieves but in defects in the social system. To be sure, the ultimate causes of these defects may be the bad character—the sin—of the movers and shakers of society. The causes of the problem, in any event, often lie at a considerable distance from its symptoms.

This systemic view of social problems implies that solutions must also be systemic. I use the term "systemic" advisedly, because the medical metaphor of a systemic infection is one that Hythloday himself employs in summarizing his views on social problems, near the end of Book I: applying a topical remedy at the point of the symptom may block the manifestation of the problem at that point, but, Hythloday says, "while you are intent upon the cure of one part, you make worse the malady of the other parts" (105/39–107/1–2). The true remedies for a problem such as theft will take the form of legal and institutional changes designed to eliminate its causes. Hythloday suggests a series of such changes: "Make laws that the destroyers of farm-steads and country villages should either restore them or hand them over to people who will restore them. . . . Restrict this right of rich individuals to buy up everything and this license to exercise a kind of monopoly for themselves. Let fewer be brought up in idleness. Let farming be resumed and let cloth-working be restored . . ." (69/38–71/5).

As has been pointed out several times, this systemic analysis is greatly in advance of most of the social theorizing of More's era.[4] It strikes us as one of the most modern aspects of his book, anticipating not only the elaborate causal analysis that we expect from social planners but the understanding that solutions to social problems are to be sought in well-designed legal and institutional adjustments, not in moralistic condemnation of the consequences of the problems. (Not that our time is devoid of views like that of Hythloday's opponent.) Moreover, it is clear that this object lesson in the analysis and solution of social problems is highly appropriate in a book on the best condition of the commonwealth; and, beyond that, one can see that Hythloday's argument that thorough reform can be effected only by large systemic changes prepares us for the account of Utopia, where many European problems have been eliminated by a radical reordering of the social system.

There is yet another way, less obvious to a modern reader, in which Book I prepares us for Book II. In answer to the question why the problem of theft continues unabated despite the execution of so many thieves, Hythloday immediately asserts that the reason is that executing thieves is neither moral nor expedient: "You need not wonder, for this manner of punishing thieves goes beyond justice and is not for the public good" (61/17–18).[5] It is this point that his elaborate causal analysis is concerned to establish. Hythloday's second disquisition at Morton's—his response to the Cardinal's request that he offer an alternative punishment for theft—is structured by the same considerations. The current English policy is, first, "altogether unjust" (73/9)—a point that he argues at some length. Second, it is inexpedient: "Besides, surely everyone knows how absurd and even dangerous to the commonwealth it is that a thief and a murderer should receive the same punishment . . ." (75/5–7).

As More's contemporaries would have recognized, this strategy of argument has its origin in rhetorical theory. In many respects, More was a typical Renaissance humanist. What this primarily means is that he was trained in an educational tradition centered in a revived classical rhetoric.[6] Rhetoric, originally the art of making persuasive speeches, had deeply influenced the art of literary composition in general, for which it offered detailed rules. For one thing, it divided compositions into genres, and gave lists of subject-matter headings, called "topoi"—topics—that have proved useful in developing arguments in the different genres. These topics provided, in effect, a "grid of issues"[7] upon which arguments could be plotted, and, as such, they were extremely influential in giving shape to discourse from the classical era down to the beginning of our own century.

Since the subject of Hythloday's remarks at Morton's is the advisability or inadvisability of a particular policy, his speeches belong to one of the three great genres of classical oratory: deliberative, the oratory of persuasion and dissuasion. The central topics of deliberative are *honestas* and *utilitas*—honor and expediency (or, less pejoratively, usefulness).[8] The deliberative orator, that is, normally argues that a particular course of action is advisable on the ground that it is honorable, or on the ground that it is expedient—or argues that it is *in*advisable, as being either dishonorable or inexpedient. Naturally, the strongest case is made when it can be shown that considerations of honor and expediency point in the same direction.

Hythloday clearly won the debate at Morton's, but his use of the episode as an exemplum fails to convince More and Giles of the inutility of sending humanist sages to court. The point of the exemplum, according to Hythloday, lies in the fact that Morton's courtiers were wholly unreceptive to Hythloday's suggestions—until the Cardinal himself expressed qualified approval of them. These courtiers, Hythloday thinks, are typical of the advisers who surround those in power, and, as this story shows, they are such self-serving sycophants that it is impossible for any genuine exchange of ideas to take place among them: so what is the use of joining a royal council? But More is not convinced (perhaps because he has noticed, like many readers of the episode, that the only *real* royal councilor present—Morton—is ideally responsive to the new ideas). Undaunted, Hythloday proceeds to give two further examples, this time of imaginary privy council meetings (87–97). Privy councils are of course deliberative bodies, and Hythloday's accounts of these meetings consist of summaries of a series of deliberative orations structured, again, by the topics of honor and expediency; there are brief summaries of the speeches of the other councilors, who consider only *utilitas,* and longer ones of Hythloday's own speeches, which consult *honestas* as well. The councils deal, respectively, with foreign and domestic policy. Foreign policy turns out to mean a collection of stratagems by which the king can get hold of as much of other kings' territory as possible; domestic policy means a collection of stratagems by which the king can maximize the intake of his treasury. In both councils, Hythloday imagines himself as rising to maintain that these stratagems are both dishonorable and self-defeating. This time his point is that although this is the kind of advice kings *should* get, and the kind that he would have to give if he were to become a royal adviser, it is foolish to think that such counsels would have any effect in such a context. "To sum it all up," as he says to More and Giles at the end of his account, "if I tried to obtrude these and like ideas on men strongly inclined to the opposite way of thinking, to what deaf ears should I tell the tale [97/35–38]!"

Hythloday's arguments to More and Giles, his remarks at Morton's, and his speeches in the imaginary privy council meetings are all, then, shaped in accordance with the precepts of deliberative oratory, by examining policies in terms of the twin topics of *honestas* and *utilitas*. Given More's passion for rhetoric—which is manifested in many virtuoso orations in and out of literary works throughout his career—this fact is not surprising. What *is* surprising about Hythloday's use of the topics of deliberative, and what would have been conspicuous to readers trained in rhetoric, is that in all the subjects he discusses he insists that honor and expediency point in the same direction. Honor does not require that the sage attach himself to a ruler's council, because such a course is not really advantageous to the commonwealth. The English policy for dealing with theft is both immoral and self-defeating; and the same is true of the supposedly expedient policies recommended by the other councilors in the imaginary privy council meetings. The truly expedient policy in all these cases is one that is consistent with the dictates of morality and religion. We get the strong impression that Hythloday would say the same about any issue.

In this respect he dissents sharply from the classical rhetoricians. For they, though always preferring to argue that honor and expediency bid the same, recognize that in some situations the orator will have to argue that expediency—or (better) "necessity," the third great topic of deliberative—requires that a dishonorable course be followed, and in still others will have to argue that honor demands that a very costly, even ruinous, course be followed.[9] But Hythloday, though happy to use rhetorical precepts, is, as the opening pages of Book I make clear, not a rhetorician but a philosopher. Moreover, though primarily interested in Greek philosophy, he finds value in "certain treatises of Seneca and Cicero" (51/3–4); that is, in Roman Stoicism. And in fact the classic statement of the position that the moral and the expedient never truly conflict is found in one of those treatises—*De officiis*—in which Cicero expounds Stoic doctrine.[10]

Indeed it is the character More who plays the orthodox rhetorician in *Utopia*—something that is clearest in the exchange that follows Hythloday's pessimistic summary of the implications of his accounts of supposedly typical council meetings. What these examples show, Hythloday says, is that there "is no room for philosophy with rulers" (99/9–10)—and thus no room for philosophers. It is true, More allows, that there is no room for "this academic philosophy which thinks that everything is suitable to every place."

> But there is another philosophy, more practical for statesmen, which knows its stage, adapts itself to the play in hand, and performs its role neatly and appropriately. . . . [Y]ou must not force upon people new and strange ideas which you realize will carry no weight with persons of opposite conviction. On the

contrary, by the indirect approach you must seek and strive to the best of your power to handle matters tactfully. What you cannot turn to good you must at least[11] make as little bad as you can [99/12–101/2].

Sometimes the only way to achieve good is by indirection, by dissimulation and compromise. These are the morally dubious, necessary means to the morally impeccable ends at which the good councilor aims. The useful is *not* always the same as the honorable.

Hythloday is unimpressed by this argument. First, he claims that the kind of accommodation More recommends simply will not work. Hythloday does not know (he says) whether a philosopher is permitted to lie. But he is certain that "By this approach . . . I should accomplish nothing else than to share the madness of others as I tried to cure their lunacy" (101/5–7). Second, he maintains that the "indirect approach" (99/38) is morally and religiously unacceptable: "Truly, if all the things which by the perverse morals of men have come to seem odd are to be dropped as unusual and absurd, we must dissemble among Christians[12] almost all the doctrines of Christ. Yet He forbade us to dissemble them . . ." (101/23–26). Once again, that is, Hythloday argues—this time in direct opposition to More—that the moral and the expedient coincide, that a morally dubious expedient is, in a true view, *in*expedient.

There is thus an extraordinary amount of attention in Book I to the question of the degree of compatibility of the useful and the moral. The question evidently interested More deeply, as it did other humanists. The claim that the moral and the expedient are identical was a standard theme of early humanist political thought, which is permeated by Stoicism; but in the fifteenth century some Italian humanists began to assert that *honestas* is not always the same as *utilitas.*[13] A couple of years before More wrote *Utopia,* Machiavelli produced, in *The Prince,* the most famous of all statements of this position. More could not have known Machiavelli's book (which was published only in 1532), but he certainly knew the tradition of thought that it crystallized.

The question of the relation of the moral and the expedient was not merely timely, though, or merely relevant to the topics debated in Book I. It also bears on the subject of the best condition of the commonwealth. If the moral and the expedient are ultimately identical, then it is theoretically possible to design a commonwealth that would always act morally. But if the moral and the expedient cannot be fully reconciled, then this ideal could never be achieved, even in theory.

The fact that More recognized the importance of this issue to the theory of the ideal commonwealth seems clear from what follows the exchange about the "indirect approach." The question of the validity of this approach is never resolved, presumably because More was genuinely of two minds about it. In the fiction, though, the question is left unresolved because More, Giles, and Hythloday get diverted into another matter. In the heat of debate, Hythloday ventures a bold confession: "Yet surely, my dear More, to tell you candidly my heart's sentiments, it appears to me that wherever you have private property and all men measure all things by cash values, there it is scarcely possible for a commonwealth to have justice or prosperity—unless you think justice exists where all the best things flow into the hands of the worst citizens or prosperity prevails where all is divided among very few . . ." (103/24–30). This is a plausible extrapolation from Hythloday's analysis of social problems: if everything is connected to everything, so that, for example, the root cause of theft by poor people is the greed of the rich, and the solution of such problems requires major changes in the social system, it is not unreasonable to conclude that communism provides the only way to social justice. Certainly this was the conclusion of the first theorist of the ideal commonwealth—Plato, whom Hythloday cites approvingly on two occasions (87/19–23, 103/16–23). And it is not only the ideal of justice that Hythloday sees as requiring the abolition of private property, but also the practical desideratum of prosperity. This is the more surprising claim—though not surprising coming from Hythloday, because it amounts, after all, to another instance of the contention that the moral and the expedient are identical. And again the character More disagrees with him:

> Life cannot be satisfactory where all things are common. How can there be a sufficient supply of goods when each withdraws himself from the labor of production? For the individual does not have the motive of personal gain and he is rendered slothful by trusting to the industry of others. Moreover, when people are goaded by want and yet the individual cannot legally keep as his own what he has gained, must there not be trouble from continual bloodshed and riot? This holds true especially since the authority of magistrates and respect for their office have been eliminated, for how there can be any place for these among men who are all on the same level I cannot even conceive [107/5–16].

These objections, which echo Aristotle's critique of the *Republic* in Book II of the *Politics,* are practical, *realpolitik* objections. More is denying, not that absolute equality is *right,* but that it is *prudent.* The commonwealth cannot be stable, prosperous, and happy without inequality. As in the matter of counsel, political necessity, considerations of *utilitas,* dictate some deviation from the morally ideal.

More would think differently, Hythloday says, if only he had been with him in Utopia. For that commonwealth embodies the equality that More thinks impractical, and yet if More could visit it, he would admit that he "had never seen a well-ordered people anywhere but there" (107/ 23). According to Hythloday, then, Utopia *is* the ideal commonwealth, and it embodies and demonstrates the consonance of the moral and the expedient. Its institutions are, he says, at once *prudentissima atque sanctissima* (102/27–28)— most prudent *and* most holy.

This, then, is the context in which Hythloday's account of Utopia is introduced: a dispute about the degree of compatibility of the moral and the expedient, and in particular whether the ideal of equality is compatible with stability and prosperity. This context suggests that the imaginary commonwealth constitutes some kind of *test* of the degree of compatibility of *honestas* and *utilitas*; that, whatever else it may be, it also constitutes an attempt to answer this fundamental theoretical question about the best condition of the commonwealth: Is it possible, even theoretically, for a commonwealth to be at once *prudentissima* and *sanctissima,* both shrewd and holy?

To answer this question, More constructed Utopia by following the rules for designing an ideal commonwealth set forth in the political works of Plato and Aristotle. What it is vital to understand about these works, and what More clearly did understand, is that for Plato and Aristotle designing an ideal commonwealth is not simply a matter of piling together seemingly ideal features of a polis. The quintessential manifestation of the rationalism of Greek political thought, the best-commonwealth exercise inaugurated by Plato and refined by Aristotle has two premises: first, that the goal of the commonwealth is the happiness of its citizens; second, that the governing design principle is that of αὐτάρκεια, self-sufficiency: the best commonwealth will be one that includes everything that is necessary to the happiness of its citizens, and nothing else. From these premisses, Plato and Aristotle developed a tight four-step procedure for designing an ideal commonwealth.[14] First, it is necessary to determine what constitutes the happiest life for the individual. This is the central question of ethical theory, and, as Aristotle explains at the beginning of Book VII of the *Politics,* its answer constitutes the starting point of political theory: "Before we can undertake properly the investigation of . . . the nature of an ideal constitution . . . it is necessary for us first to determine the nature of the most desirable way of life. As long as that is obscure, the nature of the ideal constitution must also remain obscure" (1323A).[15] Second, from these conclusions about the most desirable life for the individual, the theorist derives the communal goals whose attainment will maximize the happiness of the citizens. Third, it is necessary to form a sort of checklist of the physical and institutional components that the commonwealth will have to include in order to achieve its goals. A certain amount of population will be required, and a certain kind and extent of territory; certain occupational functions will have to be performed; and so on.[16] Finally, the fourth step is to determine the particular form that each of these components should be given in order to ensure that, collectively, they will constitute the best polis, that self-sufficient system that achieves the ultimate goal of happiness for its citizens.

In the present context, what we should especially notice about this method is that its end product is a blueprint for a commonwealth characterized by perfect expediency: all that is ever considered is what will make the citizens of the polis happy, what is useful to that end. Though that which makes them happy may also be honorable, honor is not in itself a goal of the polis. This being the case, constructing such an imaginary commonwealth can provide a perfect test of the degree of compatibility of the honorable and the expedient: one merely has to observe to what extent the behavior of this commonwealth is consonant with the norms of honor, of morality and religion.

These considerations suggest the solution to the much-discussed problem of why More made Utopia non-Christian. More and all his contemporaries—including Machiavelli—knew that moral, and Christian, behavior is advisable on suprarational, religious grounds. One of the liveliest questions in early–sixteenth-century political thought, though, is that raised in Book I of *Utopia*: How far, in political life, is this kind of behavior advisable, or inadvisable, on purely prudential grounds? More realized that this question could be answered by seeing what a society pursuing perfect expediency through perfectly rational calculations would be like.

All the same, Book II of *Utopia* does not look much like Plato's *Republic* or Aristotle's *Politics*. This is because, whereas Plato and Aristotle are content to present their *reasonings* on the subject of the perfectly expedient commonwealth, More, exhibiting the rhetorician's characteristic preference for examples, gives a model of a commonwealth that embodies the *results* of his reasonings. In this, he is in fact closer to Plato's unfinished *Critias* than to the *Republic*. In the *Critias,* which was intended as a sequel to the *Republic,* Critias was to have given a narrative account of ancient Athens, imagined as the ideal commonwealth discussed in the *Republic*.

More's decision to present his results in the form of an

account of a supposedly existing commonwealth entailed suppressing or disguising the various components of the dialectical substructure of his model—its generative postulates and the arguments involved in the four steps of the best-commonwealth exercise. But once it is recognized that Book II of *Utopia* does in fact embody the results of a best-commonwealth exercise performed according to the Greek prescription, some otherwise mystifying aspects of the work become clear. In particular, this insight tells us how to take the long, not to say tedious, account of Utopian moral philosophy (161–79); and it can provide an answer to the difficult question that I posed in starting out: Why did More portray a commonwealth that is partly attractive and partly not?

The passage on moral philosophy is in fact the cornerstone of the Utopian edifice: it embodies the first step of the best-commonwealth exercise, the determination of the best life for the individual.[17] Given More's fictional form of presentation, the passage can be introduced only as incidental information about the Utopians' philosophy; but in reality it is the only substantial fossil, so to speak, of the dialectics that underlay the construction of Utopia. Since his conclusions differ in some highly significant ways from those of his Greek predecessors, and since all important aspects of the Utopian commonwealth follow from these conclusions, More evidently felt it important to include a full account of the reasonings that led to them.

The Utopians' view of human nature is not much different from that of Plato and Aristotle. For the Utopians as for the Greeks, the first and most obvious fact about that nature is that man is wholly self-interested. What this self-interested creature strives for is of course his own pleasure. In the *Republic,* Glaucon maintains that "self-interest . . . [is] the motive which all men naturally follow if they are not forcibly restrained by the law and made to respect each other's claims" (II, 359c),[18] and Plato lets him illustrate this point with the story of Gyges' ring. In the *Laws,* the view of man as pleasure-seeker is given heavy emphasis: "Human nature involves, above all, pleasures, pains, and desires, and no mortal animal can help being hung up dangling in the air (so to speak) in total dependence on these powerful influences. . . . what we all seek . . . [is] a predominance of pleasure over pain throughout our lives" (V, 732E–733A).[19] Similarly, the Utopians "maintain, having carefully considered and weighed the matter, that all our actions, and even the very virtues exercised in them, look at last to pleasure as their end and happiness" (167/3–6).

If there is little difference between the views of human nature in *Utopia* and in the Greek theorists, there also appears, at first, to be little between the conceptions of the best life that are based on these views. The Utopian moral philosophers maintain that pleasure is the goal of life, but they find that the most pleasurable life is that of virtue. Plato and Aristotle also conclude that man the pleasure-seeker finds his greatest pleasure in the life of virtue.[20] The Utopians, however, have a rather different conception of what constitutes the virtuous life, so in fact their conclusion in this step of the exercise is crucially different from the Greeks'.

The most striking characteristic of the Greek treatments of the life of virtue lies in the fact that the enjoyment of this life is regarded as compatible with the grossest social and economic inequities. In the ideal polis of the *Republic,* the most important component of the good life, philosophic contemplation, is restricted to the ruling class, the Guardians. And although Plato says nothing on the subject, the Republic presumably includes, like all Greek city-states, a large class of slaves, who, as inherently inferior beings, are excluded from the life of virtue—a circumstance that does not appear to cloud the serenity of either the Guardians or their creator. In fact, it is clear that the existence of laboring classes is a necessary condition of the Guardians' philosophic leisure. For his part, Aristotle matter-of-factly observes that

> the state is an association of equals, and only of equals; and its object is the best and highest life possible. The highest good is felicity; and that consists in the energy and perfect practice of goodness. But . . . this is not for all; some may share in it fully, but others can only share in it partially or cannot even share at all [Pol. VII, 1328A].

In sharp contrast, the Utopians conclude that individual felicity is incompatible with special privilege. Reason, they believe, tells us not only "to lead a life as free from care and as full of joy as possible" but also, "because of our natural fellowship, to help all other men . . . to attain that end" (163/28–31). Nature "surely bids you take constant care not so to further your own advantages as to cause disadvantages to your fellows" (165/20–22). And whereas Plato and Aristotle regard philosophic contemplation as the highest pleasure, the Utopians think that the "principal part" (175/35) of mental pleasure arises from "the practice of the virtues and the consciousness of a good life" (175/35–37). Thus the best life for the individual, the life that brings most pleasure to the self-interested pleasure-seeker man, is one lived in accordance with the moral norms of Christian culture. For the individual, at least, the Utopians believe they have proved that the expedient and the honorable are identical. Nor is there any reason to think that More doubted this conclusion.

But what of the collective, political level? If for private life morality is always the most expedient course, is this also true for the commonwealth—as Hythloday claims? For the most part, the Utopian commonwealth supports this claim. Given the Utopians' conclusions about the best life for the individual, it could not be otherwise. If the highest component of happiness is "the practice of the virtues and the consciousness of a good life," and if one's own happiness is incompatible with special privilege or with spoiling others' happiness, then it follows that the institutions of the commonwealth, whose goal is to maximize the happiness of its citizens, must be structured so as to implement in every possible way the Golden Rule. Indeed, the policies of the Utopian commonwealth, domestic and foreign, are on the whole much preferable to those of European nations, and are in many areas completely consistent with Christian standards, as those are interpreted in the writings of More and his associates.

Yet, as every reader knows, some aspects of Utopia are difficult or impossible to reconcile to these standards. To take the most disturbing of these: there is, first, the strict regimentation of Utopian life, and its drabness. And though some varieties of Christians may regard these as appropriate features of the good life, it is clear that More and his humanist circle did not. Earlier I cited Hythloday's remark that "he who cannot reform the lives of citizens in any other way than by depriving them of the good things of life must admit that he does not know how to rule free men." The remark embodies both the libertarianism and the relatively relaxed attitude toward bodily and aesthetic pleasures that characterize Erasmian humanists.[21] Of More himself, Erasmus reports approvingly that he is "by no means averse from all the things that bring harmless pleasure, be it only to the body."[22] Indeed the Utopians themselves believe that "no kind of pleasure is forbidden, provided no harm comes of it" (145/24–26). Yet in fact their life is hedged round with an extraordinary number and range of legal prohibitions, and with an elaborate network of positive and negative reinforcements designed to encourage good behavior with reward and praise and discourage bad behavior with humiliation. Moreover, there is a deadening sameness about Utopian life. The cities are made as nearly identical as possible. All citizens of the same sex and marital status wear identical clothes, all year round, unvarying for centuries (127/1–7). And Utopia seems nearly devoid of the arts.[23]

Then there are the disturbing aspects of Utopian foreign policy.[24] For the most part, the Utopians are generous toward their neighbors, among whom, for example, they distribute their surplus commodities "at a moderate price" (149/13), and to whom they are always happy to supply skillful and honest administrators (197/1–6). Furthermore, they detest war and the concept of martial glory, and, whenever war cannot be avoided, go to great lengths to minimize bloodshed on both sides and to minimize injury both to the common citizens of the enemy nation and to its territory (199–205, 215). Yet it turns out that there is a surprisingly large number of reasons why the Utopians will go to war—including to defend their allies, or "to requite and avenge injuries previously done to them" (201/11–12), and to obtain territory for colonization whenever the Utopian population exceeds the optimal number (137/7–22). Furthermore, some of their tactics in war are of very dubious morality. They "sow the seeds of dissension" (205/

27

33) among their enemies by sponsoring pretenders to the enemy throne. "If internal strife dies down, then they stir up and involve the neighbors of their enemies by reviving some forgotten claims to dominion such as kings have always at their disposal" (205/35–38). They employ mercenaries to do as much of their fighting as possible; and "Next to them they employ the forces of the people for whom they are fighting and then auxiliary squadrons of all their other friends. Last of all they add a contingent of their own citizens . . ." (209/16–18). Then, too, the mercenaries the Utopians prefer to employ are the savage Zapoletans, whose use is hard to reconcile with the aim of minimizing the destructiveness of war. Finally, despite their compassion for the common citizens of enemy nations, the Utopians enslave the defenders (presumably not all of them professional soldiers) of conquered cities (215/15–18); indeed, they apparently enslave *all* "[p]risoners of war . . . captured in wars fought by the Utopians themselves" (185/16–18).

The explanation of these discrepancies between Utopian practices and Christian ideals does not, I think, lie in More's having unaccountably decided to interject some passages covertly satirizing European practices in the middle of a description of a commonwealth that is in other respects much superior to European ones.[25] Instead, the explanation lies in the fact that More built Utopia by following the rules of the Greek best-commonwealth exercise, and that he was such a realistic and acute performer of that exercise.

One manifestation of More's realism is found in his wholly un-wishful view of human nature, and in the way in which this view is reflected in the structure of Utopian society. As I noted above, the Utopians conclude that man is a self-interested pleasure-seeker; nor is there anything in either book of *Utopia* to contradict this view. The Utopians also believe, of course, that man finds his greatest pleasure in the exercise of reason and virtue, and they have designed their educational system to inculcate a taste for such superior pleasure. They "regard concern for their [children's] morals and virtue as no less important than for their advancement in learning" (229/10–11); the Utopians' contempt of false pleasure has been "conceived partly from their upbringing, being reared in a commonwealth whose institutions are far removed from [such] follies . . . , and partly from instruction and reading good books" (159/3–6). Consequently, the average of human behavior in Utopia is considerably higher than in the rest of the world. Yet even in Utopia, with its splendid education, More thinks it necessary to provide a system of criminal justice: human nature is such that, no matter what nurture it receives, some fraction of individuals will always be criminals. And even those who are *not* criminals require an elaborate system of laws and moral suasion to ensure their good behavior. This realism is in fact one of the ways in which *Utopia* differs from the products of most utopian writers, who assume that, once their splendid constitutions are in place, human nature will no longer present any problems.

The most striking example of More's realism, though, and of his insight into the problems of the commonwealth, lies in his grasp of the fact that even in the ideal commonwealth there will always be conflicts between desirable goals. The problem of conflicting goals rarely seems to bother theorists of the ideal commonwealth or writers of utopias. Thus Plato and Aristotle determine the question of the amount of material goods to be supplied to the members of the ideal polis purely on the basis of ethical considerations: What amount of such goods is most conducive to a moral life? The possibility that the optimal

29

amount of these goods might not be attainable without the sacrifice of some spiritual goods does not seem to occur to them—in part, at least, because they assume that any amount of material goods can be supplied by the labor of those inhabitants (slaves and artisans) whose happiness is not among the goals of the polis. But More is acutely aware of such conflicts, and his exploration of them constitutes perhaps his most notable achievement as a political theorist.

His awareness of the conflict of goals is first apparent in the section on Utopian moral philosophy. Utopian ethics is a strange fusion of Stoicism and Epicureanism. One of the features of Epicureanism that most interests More is the so-called "hedonic calculus," Epicurus' rules for making choices among the welter of possible pleasures. The rules are that we should always choose a greater pleasure in pref-erence to a lesser one, and that we should reject any pleasure that will eventually result in pain. This formula is dear to the Utopians, and occurs three times in one form or an-other in the passage on moral philosophy (163/8–10, 167/11–14, 177/35–36). In addition, it is clear that More thinks that the same principles should be applied to resolving con-flicts between conflicting goals at the collective, political level; and it is in terms of this insight that we should under-stand most of the unattractive features of Utopia.

More was evidently impressed by the Aristotelian objec-tions to egalitarianism that he puts into his own mouth at the end of Book I. Utopia does not in fact suffer from the chaos that the character More had predicted—"must there not be trouble from continual bloodshed and riot?" (107/12)—but this is partly because a good deal of freedom has been traded off for the elaborate system of constraints (and the strict and ritualized patriarchy) of Utopia.[26] The Uto-pians, like their creator, believe in freedom. But since they

fear that unbridled freedom would threaten the stability
and security of the commonwealth—which has to be the
goal of highest priority—they are forced to curtail freedom
severely. Similar considerations account for the drabness,
the dismal uniformity, of Utopian life. It is not that such
drabness is regarded as desirable in itself: as I pointed out
above, the Utopians believe that "no kind of pleasure is
forbidden, provided no harm comes of it." The proviso
here suggests the true explanation, which lies in More's
evident conviction that the unrestricted production of the
material and aesthetic goods that would make Utopian life
more vivid would seriously compromise the achievement
of more important goals. Labor in Utopia is restricted to
"only as few crafts as natural needs and conveniences require" (131/16–17),[27] in order that as much time as possible
be devoted to "the freedom and culture of the mind" (135/
23). Moreover, as Edward Surtz remarks (387n), "The emphasis on uniformity in outward matters in Utopia appears
to be motivated by the conviction that individuality in such
matters almost inevitably becomes occasion for emulation,
vanity, and pride." Of course we may feel that the Utopians, like some other nations, have miscalculated the necessary trade-offs. Perhaps not so *much* freedom need be
sacrificed to stability; and it would seem that greater di-
versity in the forms of necessary goods and more production of artistic goods would contribute importantly to
mental pleasure. But the Utopians, we recall, hold the principal part of pleasure to "arise from the practice of the
virtues and the consciousness of a good life," and the hedonic calculus demands that no greater pleasure be sacrificed to the attainment of a lesser one.

Similar considerations explain the distressing Utopian
practices in foreign policy. It is not an accident that the

Utopians' most problematic behavior takes place beyond their borders. The object of the best-commonwealth exercise is to create a self-sufficient polity that secures the good life for its citizens. What bearing this attempt may have on the lives of people outside the best commonwealth—or even inside it, if they are not citizens—is not its concern. This is perfectly clear in the ideal commonwealths of Plato and Aristotle, whose attitude toward foreigners resembles their attitude toward slaves and artisans.[28] Presumably this is not an acceptable position for thinkers in the Stoic–Christian tradition, for whom the concept of universal human brotherhood underlies the central moral norm. Yet there is a deeply disturbing conflict here. The internal arrangements of Utopia or any other commonwealth will not really matter unless the commonwealth can be made secure; and as long as other commonwealths are not utopian it is hard to see how to secure it without indulging in some practices with respect to one's neighbors that are expedient but certainly not moral.

Evidently this problem, and the general problem of the conflict of valid goals, troubled More greatly. Surely this is why the account of Utopia not merely includes, but insists on, makes conspicuous, a number of unattractive Utopian practices; and this also helps to explain why More peppered his book with jokes, which serve to distance him (and his readers) from Utopia. On the evidence of this superbly performed best-commonwealth exercise, Hythloday is wrong on his main point: in the governance of the commonwealth, the moral is *not* always the same as the expedient. Only in a world-state, where *all* are citizens and siblings, would the identity of the moral and the expedient always hold. But, given man's fallen nature, that City of God cannot be realized until the end of time. "For," as

More says to Hythloday in their debate on the indirect approach, "it is impossible that all should be well unless all men were good, a situation which I do not expect for a great many years to come" (101/2–3).

NOTES

1. Since delivering this paper, I have had occasion to recross some of the same ground in the Introduction to *Utopia*, edd. George M. Logan and Robert M. Adams, Cambridge Texts in the History of Political Thought (Cambridge: Cambridge University Press, forthcoming). Some passages of the paper appear in revised form in that Introduction; and in turn the Introduction has supplied some rephrasings to this version of the paper.

2. See "'Si Hythlodaeo Credimus': Vision and Revision in Thomas More's *Utopia*," in *Essential Articles for the Study of Thomas More*, edd. R. S. Sylvester and G. P. Marc'hadour (Hamden, Conn.: Archon, 1977), pp. 291–92. Sylvester's article originally appeared in *Soundings*, 51 (1968), 272–89.

3. The Logan–Adams edition not yet having appeared, I quote *Utopia* from the Yale edition: *Utopia*, edd. Edward Surtz, s.j., and J. H. Hexter, The Yale Edition of Complete Works of St. Thomas More 4 (New Haven and London: Yale University Press, 1965).

4. See Russell Ames, *Citizen Thomas More and His Utopia* (Princeton: Princeton University Press, 1949), pp. 176–77; Robert P. Adams, *The Better Part of Valor: More, Erasmus, Colet, and Vives, on Humanism, War, and Peace, 1496–1535* (Seattle: University of Washington Press, 1962), pp. 125–26; J. H. Hexter, *More's* UTOPIA: *The Biography of an Idea* (Princeton: Princeton University Press, 1952), pp. 62–66, 110–12, and *Utopia*, pp. c–cii; George M. Logan, *The Meaning of More's* UTOPIA (Princeton: Princeton University Press, 1983), pp. 57–74.

5. His remarks conclude with a statement of the same point: "Such justice is more showy than really just or beneficial [*utilem*]" (71/10–11).

6. On the place of rhetoric in humanism, see especially Paul Oskar Kristeller, *Renaissance Thought: The Classic, Scholastic, and Hu-*

manist Strains (New York: Harper Torchbooks, 1961), pp. 3–23; Jerrold E. Seigel, *Rhetoric and Philosophy in Renaissance Humanism: The Union of Eloquence and Wisdom, Petrarch to Valla* (Princeton: Princeton University Press, 1968); Nancy S. Struever, *The Language of History in the Renaissance: Rhetoric and Historical Consciousness in Florentine Humanism* (Princeton: Princeton University Press, 1970); William J. Bouwsma, *The Culture of Renaissance Humanism,* American Historical Association Pamphlets, No. 401 (Washington, D.C.: American Historical Association, 1973); George M. Logan, "Substance and Form in Renaissance Humanism," *The Journal of Medieval and Renaissance Studies,* 7 (1977), 1–34; John F. Tinkler, "Renaissance Humanism and the *genera eloquentiae,*" *Rhetorica,* 5 (1987), 279–309.

7. The phrase is John F. Tinkler's, in an unpublished paper. Cf. his "Humanism as Discourse: Studies in the Rhetorical Culture of Renaissance Humanism, Petrarch to Bacon," Ph.D. Diss., Queen's University, Canada, 1983.

8. Cicero, *Inv.* 2.51.156–58, *Part. or.* 24.83–89, *De or.* 2.72.334–36, *Rhetorica ad Herennium* 3.2.3; Quintilian, *Inst. orat.* 3.8.1, 13, 22–25.

9. Cf., e.g., Cicero, *Part. or.* 25.89, *De or.* 2.82.335; Quintilian, *Inst. orat.* 3.8.1–2.

10. See, e.g., 3.3.11, 3.7.34, 3.12.49–50.

11. "At least" (*saltem*), omitted from the Yale translation, is inserted from the Addenda and Corrigenda included in *Responsio ad Lutherum* II, ed. John M. Headley, The Yale Edition of the Complete Works of St. Thomas More 5 (New Haven and London: Yale University Press, 1976), pp. 1029–36.

12. "Among Christians" is inserted from the Addenda and Corrigenda.

13. See Quentin Skinner, *The Foundations of Modern Political Thought,* 2 vols. (Cambridge: Cambridge University Press, 1978), I, 48, 125–27.

14. See Logan, *The Meaning of More's* UTOPIA, pp. 130–36. On happiness as the goal of the commonwealth, see Plato, *Rep.* IV, 420c, and *Laws* V, 743c; Aristotle, *Pol.* VII, 1324a. On αὐτάρκεια, *Rep.* II, 369b; *Pol.* VII, 1326b.

15. Quoted from *The Politics of Aristotle,* trans. Ernest Barker (Oxford: Clarendon, 1948).

16. See Plato, *Rep.* II, 369B–373D, and *Laws* V, 737C–D; Aristotle, *Pol.* VII, 1325B–1328B.

17. For a full treatment, see my *Meaning of More's* UTOPIA, pp. 144–87.

18. I quote from *The Republic,* trans. Desmond Lee, 2nd ed. (Harmondsworth: Penguin Books, 1974).

19. Trans. Trevor J. Saunders, rev. ed. (Harmondsworth: Penguin Books, 1975).

20. See, e.g., Plato, *Rep.* IX, 583A–592A, and *Laws* II, 662D, V, 732E–733A; Aristotle, *Eth. Nic.* X, 1175B–1178A, and *Pol.* VII, 1323B, VIII, 1338A.

21. See, for example, Erasmus' "The Epicurean," in *The Colloquies of Erasmus,* trans. Craig R. Thompson (Chicago: The University of Chicago Press, 1965), pp. 535–51, esp. 547–51.

22. *The Correspondence of Erasmus: Letters 993 to 1121, 1519–1520,* trans. R. A. B. Mynors, Collected Works of Erasmus 7 (Toronto, Buffalo, and London: University of Toronto Press, 1987), p. 17.

23. See James Binder, "More's *Utopia* in English: A Note on Translation," in *Essential Articles,* edd. Sylvester and Marc'hadour, pp. 229–33 (originally published in *Modern Language Notes,* 62 [1947], 370–76).

24. On this topic, see Schlomo Avineri, "War and Slavery in More's *Utopia,*" *International Review of Social History*, 7 (1962), 260–90.

25. Unaccountable or not, this has been a common line of explanation. See, for example, Ames, *Citizen Thomas More,* pp. 84–85, and Edward L. Surtz, S.J., *The Praise of Wisdom: A Commentary on the Religious and Moral Problems and Backgrounds of St. Thomas More's* UTOPIA (Chicago: Loyola University Press, 1957), p. 293. Robert P. Adams shows that many of the "antichivalric" Utopian military practices are consonant with Stoic and Christian humanist ideas (*Better Part of Valor,* pp. 152–54). But this line of argument cannot explain the particular practices discussed here.

26. Cf. Hexter, *Utopia,* pp. xlii–xliv.

27. The Yale translation is altered here as suggested by Clarence H. Miller, "The English Translation in the Yale *Utopia*: Some Corrections," *Moreana* 9 (1966), 58.

28. See, e.g., *Rep.* V, 470C; *Pol.* VII, 1334A.

3

The Key to Nowhere: Pride and *Utopia*

Thomas I. White
Rider College

THOMAS MORE'S *Utopia* has been aptly described as a work that can be read in an evening but may take a lifetime to understand.[1] One reason for this is that the book is built on the intellectual equivalent of a geological fault. The simple landscape suggested by *Utopia*'s structure and conception belies subterranean forces that push and pull the book in different directions. The resulting tensions may not lead to earthquakes, but they certainly erupt in dramatically different interpretations of More's little classic.

This essay argues that these tensions can be at least partially mitigated and *Utopia*'s fundamental unity discovered through the concept of *pride*. The book's central insight involves the relationship between pride and social evil. And it is through this theme that the conceptual strain between the philosophical and the religious, and the structural tension between Books I and II, can be resolved.

37

I
OPPOSING TENDENCIES, OPPOSING INTERPRETATIONS

Thomas More's *Utopia* is a book built on a fundamental duality. As Richard Sylvester points out and George Logan reminds us, the book's very title—"Concerning the Best Condition of the Commonwealth and the New Island of Utopia"—signals this tension by suggesting that the two may not be the same. Similarly, More's masterpiece comprises two very different books. One focuses on the grim realities of social evil in sixteenth-century England, while the other describes a nearly perfect fantasy world on the other side of the globe. Even the book's author has two distinct sides. Thomas More was a successful London attorney who aspired to royal service and who probably wrote *Utopia* as part of a campaign for a position at Court. Yet this same man tested his religious vocation at the Charterhouse, would shortly begin a relentless attack against heresy, and would ultimately die as a martyr to his faith.

We are faced with clearly opposing tendencies. The book is both practical and philosophical; its author, sacred and worldly. Predictably, these two tendencies surface in scholarly discussions of the book. Karl Kautsky read the book as proto-Communistic; Russell Ames retorted that it was republican. J. H. Hexter saw the work as a serious description of More's ideal society; C. S. Lewis regarded it as fiction and satire, not political theory. Literary critics like R. S. Sylvester and Elizabeth McCutcheon understand *Utopia* as a convoluted critique of its narrator, Raphael Hythloday. Disagreement extends even to the book's form, with some scholars pointing to its two parts as being so different that the whole lacks any genuine coherence. Others concede this difference, but see the parts as complementary—fitting together like two oddly shaped puzzle pieces.

The Most Recent Interpreters: Logan and Marius

Not surprisingly, polarities emerge even in *Utopia*'s most recent interpreters. George Logan links More's book to ancient and modern philosophical traditions. Richard Marius, by contrast, places *Utopia* in the context of medieval spirituality.

Logan begins by accepting the main conclusions of what he calls the "humanistic interpreters": scholars such as Edward Surtz, Russell Ames, J. H. Hexter, Robert P. Adams, Fritz Caspari, and Quentin Skinner. He writes:

> the researches of the humanistic interpreters have served to establish fundamental guidelines for the interpretation of the book as a whole, by proving beyond any reasonable doubt that *Utopia* is a careful and essentially serious work, and that its primary disciplinary affiliation is with the tradition of political theory. These points have been established, first, by the demonstration that, far from being a revel of unconstrained invention, *Utopia* reflects More's painstaking collection and fusion of ideas from a wide range of books, especially serious works of political thought. . . . Second, the humanistic interpreters have narrowed the spectrum of possible ironic readings of *Utopia* by showing that most of the social, political, and religious ideas of the book were regarded with genuine approval by More.[2]

Placing *Utopia* in the context of serious political theory, Logan sees the book as More's attempt to compete with Plato and Aristotle in the classical "best-commonwealth exercise." And pointing to More's methodology, Logan awards the palm to the English humanist.[3]

Furthermore, Logan argues that *Utopia*'s coherence is fashioned from a debate in classical rhetoric about the relationship between *honestas* and *utilitas* (honor and expediency). Logan claims that throughout Book I Hythloday departs from the view of the classical rhetoricians and argues (like the Stoic philosophers) for their identity.[4] In Logan's view, Book II's description of an "ideal" society with a number of less than ideal features, then, serves as More's challenge to his own narrator. As Logan explains, "in the governance of the commonwealth, the moral is *not* always the same as the expedient."[5]

Richard Marius, however, dwells on More's brooding, religious disposition. *Utopia* then becomes less an intellectual exercise and more a discourse on restraining the dark forces of sin.[6] Recognizing More's obvious use of social and political institutions described in the pages of Plato and Aristotle, Marius nonetheless claims that More ultimately patterned his ideal community after a religious institution. "Those who say that Utopian society is the monastery extended to whole families," he explains, "are much closer to the mark than those who see it as a book of serious political theory. . . . Behind [More's] model [of a good community] was a pattern of thought that was utterly Christian and medieval."[7]

Good Learning or Taming Sin?

And so nearly five centuries after *Utopia*'s composition and thousands of pages of modern scholarship later, we are again faced with very different readings of More's great book. In reality, however, these two interpretations are complementary. For each scholar captures an important dimension of *Utopia* that the other misses. And the gap between them is bridged by More's concern with the sin of pride.

Logan is correct in seeing that More wrote his book for a humanistic audience and self-consciously draws both specific facts and general inspiration from ancient political philosophy. But Logan gives insufficient attention to the fact that the Greeks saw political theory as a branch of moral philosophy, a sentiment that Thomas More would share if only to play by the same rules in his competition against the ancients in what Logan calls the "best-commonwealth exercise."

We can be quite sure, however, that More sincerely believed in the connection between political and ethical issues. And even more important is the fact that More regarded the connection between ethics and religion to be just as firm. Thomas More, like his Utopians, would never discuss ethics independently of religion. And Logan's failure to address this connection weakens his interpretation. In particular, Logan's argument that *Utopia* is unified by More's consideration of the secular concepts *honestas* and *utilitas* is ultimately incomplete.

And this is where we find the strength of Marius' reading of More's book. For Marius is absolutely correct in linking More's ruminations about an ideal society to his religious sensibilities. Marius draws a convincing picture of Thomas More as a man whose mind could not help but move from social planning to sin. As a devout sixteenth-century Christian, Thomas More differs greatly from Plato or Aristotle. Philosophers ancient and modern have no trouble separating ethics from religion. Not so Thomas More.

Utopia clearly demonstrates More's belief in the utility of the social and political wisdom of the ancients. But it shows just as clearly that More's ultimate standard for appraising classical philosophy is its value in combating sin in society. And for Thomas More, the chief sin is *pride*. The distance between Logan and Marius, then, is bridged by the fact that in the mind of Thomas More social and political theory would invariably lead to ethics and thereby to religion. Or, to be more precise, More would naturally go from Plato to pride.

II
PRIDE

There is nothing novel, of course, about saying that pride is central to *Utopia*. Raphael Hythloday blasts the vice in his peroration, and pride's importance is frequently recognized in interpretations of *Utopia*. But these discussions are as unsatisfactory as they are frequent. For example, J. H. Hexter writes: "Once we recognize that More's analysis of sixteenth century society led him to the conclusion that pride was the source of the greater part of its ills, the pattern of the Utopian commonwealth becomes clear, consistent, and intelligible. In its fundamental structure it is a great social instrument for the subjugation of pride."[8] But Hexter never tells us what More really means by pride, why his "great social instrument" focuses so much on the society's *institutions,* or how the humanist could realistically build his entire Utopian edifice on this single sin.

Thus, to appreciate fully the central role of the concept and thereby to see how pride actually can tie together such disparate discussions as Books I and II, it is necessary to get a precise sense of what Thomas More has in mind when he refers to pride. Only then will we be able to see how pride drives Book I and leads More to combat it by focusing on his imaginary society's institutions. That is, only then will it make sense to say that pride is the central concept around which the entire book turns.

Pride as the Source of Social Evil

Any discussion of *Utopia* should keep clearly in mind More's primary aim in writing the book. It may be accurate to say that More was imitating Plato, competing with the ancients in a "best-commonwealth exercise," demonstrating the moral and political utility of ancient philosophy or attacking pride. It is also true that the book is ironic, satiric, humorous, and a literary *tour de force*. But none of these explanations is fundamental enough.

Utopia's primary aim is *to show the source of social evil*. That this is More's aim is stated by individuals who were in a position to know best—Erasmus and Peter Giles, More's two friends most closely connected with *Utopia*'s composition and publication. Both men offer testimony that More was looking to show the source of evil in commonwealths. In his famous letter to Ulrich von Hutten, Erasmus explains that "[More] published his *Utopia* for the purpose of showing what are the things that occasion mischief in commonwealths . . . ," and Giles echoes this in his prefatory letter to Busleyden when he praises "the sagacity with which [More] has noted the sources from which all evils actually arise in the commonwealth. . . ."[9]

When we first look at *Utopia* in this light, More seems to point to a series of unsurprising factors: injustice, greed, royal ambition for conquest. Of course, when Raphael fo-

43

cuses on private property, More seems to be on his way to saying that there is *one* primary source of social evil, and that it is *economic*. However, we must see that while More does settle on one primary cause of harm in societies, it is not an institution—private property—but an attitude: *pride*.

If we asked Thomas More, then, what *Utopia* tells us is the chief source of social evil, his answer would unquestionably be *"Pride!" Utopia* climaxes with a blistering speech about wealth and poverty in which Raphael Hythloday, More's philosophical narrator, insists that *pride* is the main factor responsible for economic injustice and for keeping sixteenth-century Europe from reforming itself. Pride is not just *one* source of social evil, but *the* source—"the prince and parent of all plagues."[10]

The great danger of pride so struck More that he dwells on it in writings throughout his life. The *Four Last Things* (1522) identifies pride as "the sin that is the very head and root of all sins . . . the mischievous mother of all manner vice."[11] *A Treatise on the Passion* (1534) labels it "of al synne the prynce" and reports that pride caused both the fall of Satan and the Fall of Man.[12] Furthermore, More points out that he has "seen many vices ere this that at the first seemed far from pride, and yet well considered to the uttermost it would well appear that of that root they sprang."[13] "This cursed root of pride," he observes, "[spreadeth] his branches into all other kinds, besides his proper malice for his own part."[14]

Pride is central to *Utopia* because for Thomas More it is absolutely central in the realm of sin. In More's mind it is impossible to overemphasize pride's importance and its great dangers to both the individual and society.

The Nature and Danger of Pride

Utopia's major aim, then, is to show how pride is the chief source of evil in societies. But precisely what does More mean by "pride"?

Of course, to the modern ear, "pride" has a positive ring. We say that we are proud of our accomplishments or our children. "Pride" has come to mean something akin to healthy self-approval. However, when Thomas More speaks of pride he means something quite negative—a cardinal sin—what we today call a kind of insufferable "arrogance." More important than what we call this trait, however, is that Thomas More sees that it is created by a particular set of conditions.

Interestingly enough, despite pride's importance in *Utopia*, we have to look elsewhere to find out what More really means by it and where it comes from. *Utopia* tells us how dangerous pride is, identifies the major conditions conducive to it, and offers remedies for it. But the book does not really describe the heart of the vice.

The initial descriptions of pride are not especially surprising. In the *Four Last Things* More refers to it as "an high estimation of ourselves"[15] and in the *Treatise on the Passion* as the "delite and lyking of oure selfe."[16] But liking oneself hardly seems very dangerous.

The key to the sin, however, is contained in the fact that pride is what we might call a social vice. More does not mean a private "delight of self" or personal feelings of self-satisfaction. The attitude More decries requires other people and is always at someone else's expense. It is not just feeling good about yourself. It is feeling good because you feel *superior* to someone else, a fact which is captured well in the Latin *superbia* and its Greek root ὑπέρβιος.

Thomas More, then, is talking about a situation in which we feel good about ourselves only if there is someone who comes up short by comparison. As Raphael charges, "Pride measures prosperity not by her own advantages but by others' disadvantages" (243/33–38). That is why it is important to understand the attitude More is describing as a kind of arrogance. When More talks about pride, he means feeling qualitatively better than the people around us, feeling that our brethren are less human or less deserving than we are, and delighting in their inferiority and misfortune. Raphael states that "Pride would not consent to be made even a goddess if no poor wretches were left for her to domineer over and scoff at, if her good fortune might not dazzle by comparison with their miseries, if the display of her riches did not torment and intensify their poverty" (243/35–38). The essence of pride, then, is feeling superior to others and reveling in their inferiority.

Thomas More believes that two specific conditions produce such feelings. The first is clearly material—wealth. In *Utopia* More twice defines pride in material and economic terms. For example, early in Book II More tells us that pride "counts it a personal glory to excel others by superfluous display of possessions" (139/8–9; cf. 243/33–38). Similarly, in *A Dialogue of Comfort Against Tribulation* More writes that the "arrow of pride" from which the "pavice of God" protects us is "worldly wealth and prosperity."[17] More thinks that simply having more wealth than other people will tempt us to think that we are better than they are. More apparently believes that having more money than others will encourage us to think that we are entitled to it—and that we are entitled to it because we are superior to them in some fundamental way.

The second set of conditions that induce pride is less

tangible than the first, but no less dangerous—desiring glory, yearning after what More calls "the vain praise of the people," and being placed in authority over others.[18] More thinks that having power over others or receiving the adulation of the crowd will also encourage us to think that there is some basic difference between us and the people who either are praising us or are under us. Thus, More is wary about any condition that could lead one person to think that he is better than another, seeing these as circumstances that would probably engender that "delight and liking of self" which is pride.

It is important to note at this point that More does not attack wealth, power, or any other specific condition per se. Indeed, he believes that used properly each of these can produce considerable good. The problem lies in what encourages people to misuse them. Unfortunately, More seems to suggest that simply having them predisposes people to do more harm than good because of the feelings produced.

But what is it that makes such feelings of self-satisfaction and superiority so dangerous? Can having more money, power, or praise than the people around us really produce a feeling that is the "mother of all manner of vice" and "the prince and parent of all plagues"? Can such an attitude of superiority really wreak havoc in a society?

For Thomas More, the answer is clearly "Yes." And the harm comes from such arrogance in two ways. First, the feelings of superiority alone are dangerous. After all, practices ranging from theft to manipulating and deceiving people to racism to terrorism frequently involve a belief in the fundamental human superiority of the aggressor and the human inferiority of the victim. Compounding matters, however, is the fact that the proud do not remain satisfied with the original inequality that is responsible for their feelings of superiority. Instead, they use their superior wealth and power to get even more, thereby creating an even greater inequality between themselves and others.

III
PRIDE AND *Utopia*

Once *Utopia* is seen as an essay on pride, the entire work takes on a new and more unified look. Instead of finding a debate about councilorship and critique of greed and ambition followed by an account of a fantasy society, we discover that both books of *Utopia* can be seen to have pride as a central theme. Book I then becomes an account of the harm pride causes in society, and Book II contains a program for defusing the vice.

Pride's Harm: Book I

Thomas More's belief in the connection between pride and social evil is a central theme of Book I of *Utopia*. As is More's way, he makes his point more by drawing a picture than by explaining it. And in Book I he sketches various views of the evil that pride works.[19] Much of this, of course, is connected with Raphael's reasons for resisting the suggestion by More and Giles that he should become a councilor to some monarch. The heart of Hythloday's argument is that he could not thereby promote the public interest, as the two humanists suppose. Monarchs are more concerned with waging war, he claims, and councilors with preserving their pretensions of being wiser than anyone around them. As if to instruct his audience in the point of his story immediately before describing the scene at Morton's court, Raphael labels the attitude of these courtiers "*proud* [*superba*], ridiculous, and obstinate" (59/16; emphasis added).

Raphael begins by showing how the political and economic conditions in sixteenth-century England foster poverty, theft, and idleness, with the wool trade in particular forcing people off the land. When Raphael recommends that the Polylerites' treatment of thieves is more just and practical than the English practice of hanging them, the lawyer with whom he is debating rejects the idea out of hand.[20] The privy council of the French king is then portrayed as plotting how to expand his kingdom by using deception, bribery, and intrigue. And councilors of "some king or other" are described as more intent on hatching schemes to increase the royal treasury than on how the king should care for his people.[21]

The social ills that Hythloday recounts are so serious and deeply rooted that Raphael makes the radical suggestion of destroying the primary institution that makes material inequality and its dangerous offspring, pride, possible in the first place. Hythloday's well-known claim is that " 'I am fully persuaded that no just and even distribution of goods can be made and that no happiness can be found in human affairs unless private property is utterly abolished' " (105/18–21).

Book I's central theme, then, is that people with money and power are concerned only with getting more of each. They are oblivious to the harm they do to others, or, like the lawyer in Morton's court, they heartlessly and foolishly contend that the poor and wretched are the authors of their own misery. Contemporary Europe is shown to be rife with poverty, cruelty, injustice, greed, and self-interest. As we saw above, all this is in keeping with Thomas More's understanding of the effects of pride.

Pride Combated: Book II

If Book I shows the contemporary crop of evils that grows from pride, Book II suggests how pride might be combated. Since certain specific conditions can induce dangerous feelings of self-importance and superiority, the key is to structure society so as to prevent those conditions from existing. With this in mind, it is especially significant that after observing that "Pride is too deeply fixed in men to be easily plucked out," Raphael points to the shape of the Utopian commonwealth (*Reipublicae forma*) and their institutions (*ea vitae instituta*) as the main reasons that Utopia is such a good society (245/3–9).

How does Utopia keep its citizens' pride in check? That is, what are the conditions on More's island that keep people from developing feelings of superiority that could lead to their taking advantage of one another? Clearly, the most fundamental institution that aims to keep pride under reign is Utopian communism. (This should come as no surprise given the material and economic conditions that More believes lead to the vice.) Raphael claims that the lack of private property and the even distribution of goods is the key to the Utopians' happiness. This obviously prevents the accumulation of wealth or material goods in a way that allows anyone to see that his life is significantly different from anyone else's from a material standpoint. Thus, the entire Utopian economy is shaped to stem the development of unwarranted feelings of "delight and liking of self."

But since it is not just wealth and prosperity that are dangerous, we also find other precautions against pride in Utopia. First, we find them in the political domain, where anything that brings either special attention or special treatment to the individual officials is checked. Campaigning for office is forbidden. Officials' living conditions are only slightly better than those of the rest of the citizenry. The officials' power is restricted so that it will be used for the public good, not their own interest. And the number of officials is limited so that the dangers of the temptations which come from political responsibility are restricted to a small group. Such conditions make it difficult for them to develop a conception of themselves that separates them very much from the rest of the population.

The same idea governs a variety of social practices. Institutions are shaped so that people are discouraged from thinking of themselves as especially different from one another. Whenever possible there are no signs of distinction or status symbols. Their clothes are similar, the houses are all the same, and they are even exchanged by lot every decade. Praise is bestowed for being willing to put aside individual concerns in order to advance others' interests, not for being a special individual set apart from others. The overall size of the society is even regulated in order to prevent factions from developing. (After all, pride can also afflict groups, and More saw the need for preventing the possibility of one group's coming to believe that it is superior to another group.)

And the impulse to restrain pride is apparent even in Utopian religious practices. Most obviously, the Utopians' prayers work against pride. While they acknowledge God's power and thank Him for His beneficence, the prayers plant enough doubt to work against arrogance and blind dogmatism. Raphael explains that in the final prayers each Utopian thanks God

> for all the benefits received, particularly that by the divine favor
> he has chanced on that commonwealth which is the happiest
> and has received that religion which he *hopes* to be the truest.
> If he errs in these matters or if there is anything better and
> more approved by God than that commonwealth or that re-
> ligion, he prays that He will, of His goodness, bring him to
> the knowledge of it, for he is ready to follow in whatever path
> He may lead him. But if this form of a commonwealth be the
> best and his religion the truest, he prays that then He may give
> him steadfastness and bring all other mortals to the same way
> of living and the same opinion of God—*unless there be something
> in this variety of religions which delights His inscrutable will* [237/
> 14–26; emphasis added].

The Utopian economy, political traditions, social and religious institutions are all involved. That is, virtually every aspect of Utopian society is designed to discourage its citizens from thinking that they are significantly different from—that is, better than—one another. The point of all these institutions is the same—to discourage pride, to discourage the arrogance that is the hallmark of believing that we are fundamentally better than the people around us, an arrogance that leads us to treat ourselves and them differently to our advantage.

Pride: The Core of Utopia

It should now be apparent both why it is plausible to claim that pride is *Utopia*'s central concept and also exactly what that means. It should also be clear how an understanding of this fact can provide us with an interpretation that bridges the gap between those of scholars like George Logan and Richard Marius.

"Pride" is Thomas More's shorthand description of a proclivity in people to develop an insufferable arrogance when confronted with situations in which they can find someone falling short in comparison to them—especially in terms of money, esteem, or power. This arrogance first leads the individuals afflicted to regard their "superiority" as deserved and then inclines them to make it even more pronounced. Book I shows us the workings of this impulse in the sixteenth century. Book II details a society that is fashioned so as to reduce the chance of such feelings developing in the first place.

All this may be in keeping with the classical tradition of utopian speculation and with demonstrating the value of a rational, philosophical approach in searching for causes and solutions of social evil. But More relies on a religious perspective to arrive at his ultimate conclusion about the nature of social evil, a fact that demonstrates the complementary character of *Utopia*'s secular and religious dimensions.

Of course, as central as any one concept is to understanding *Utopia,* the book remains multi-layered and multi-faceted. And it would be folly to claim that all the book's complexities can be easily resolved. Nonetheless, I believe that *Utopia* takes on new coherence when viewed in light of the idea that More's understanding of pride is the ultimate seed from which the rest of the book springs.

IV
POSTSCRIPT:
WHY INSTITUTIONS?—
THE PSYCHOLOGY OF PRIDE

It is extremely significant that the institutional precautions against pride in Utopia are so extensive. As just noted, virtually every aspect of Utopian society is designed to work against pride, and that shows just how powerful a threat Thomas More saw pride to be to society.

That Thomas More saw pride as so dangerous is something we should take a moment to reflect on. After all, remember where More was in his life at this point. When he started *Utopia* in 1515, Thomas More was almost forty. He had been practicing law since the early part of the century; he began to have firsthand experience with English politics apparently as early as the Parliament of 1504; in 1510 he was appointed one of London's Under-Sheriffs; and now he was on a royal embassy. More had learned much about how the practical world operates; he was realistic and brought a good deal of practical experience to his theoretical analysis of the source of social evil. So his insights in *Utopia* about the causes of social evil should be neither taken lightly nor dismissed as an academic exercise.

It is with this in mind that we should ask the question "Why does More devote so much attention to the shape of institutions in Utopia?" After all, logically there are two ways of dealing with the fact that specific conditions produce undesirable attitudes—prevent the conditions from existing or try to change the individual's response. Why does More not try to change people by education so that they will react to good fortune with humility instead of pride? Why is his concern with the shape of the external features of society so single-minded and extensive?

It seems that More believes so strongly in regulating the shape of society's institutions—the conditions under which people live—because he thinks this is the only way to deal with the great danger that pride presents. And it is the only way because the other element of the calculation—the human personality—cannot be changed. More writes in *Utopia* that "Pride is too deeply fixed in men to be easily plucked out" (245/3). In his opinion the internal shape of the human personality is carved in stone.

This is an important psychological aspect of the insight that More offers in *Utopia* about the relationship between pride and social evil. More assumes a direct and powerful relationship between the external conditions in which we live, on the one hand, and our internal ideas, dispositions, the way we see the world, on the other. More suggests that exposing human beings to particular conditions will produce specific attitudes in us, and that this process is largely beyond our control. In short, exposure to particular material conditions affects our perception of reality.

This is first suggested at the end of Book I on the heels of Raphael's endorsement of Utopian communism. And it is important to note that the absence of private property in Utopia has the salutary effect of keeping the Utopians' minds more open than the Europeans'. In answer to the objections of More and Giles to Utopian communism, Raphael points out how much the Utopians have benefited from their encounters with other cultures. When some Romans and Egyptians were shipwrecked on Utopia, the Utopians learned everything they could from the strangers. Similarly, they drew much from Raphael and his fellows. But More's point here is the contrast with Europe. "[J]ust as they immediately at one meeting appropriated to themselves every good discovery of ours," reports Hythloday, "so I suppose it will be long before we adopt anything that is better arranged with them than with us. *This trait, I judge, is the chief reason* why, though we are inferior to them neither in brains nor in resources, their commonwealth is more wisely governed and more happily flourishing than ours" (109/14–20; emphasis added). Private property produces a clouded, self-interested mind; Utopian communism results in clearer heads. More is clearly working with the idea that there is a connection between material conditions and mental attitude.

Thomas More, then, seems to fear that if we are exposed to wealth, power, or the crowd's adulation, the way we see the world will change, and we will probably develop a dangerous sense of superiority. Furthermore, no matter how socially harmful this perspective actually is, we will not think that there is anything wrong with our ideas. In fact, More says in the *Four Last Things* that the worst type of pride—spiritual pride—amounts to seeing our vices as positive virtues.[22]

The key to this process is that we utilize some kind of psychological mechanism to justify our new perspective to ourselves. And the most likely candidate for this internal justification is what psychologists call "rationalization," that is, reinterpreting our behavior to make it seem more acceptable. So More's proud person comes up with a seemingly rational and acceptable reason for believing in and acting according to his or her own superiority and someone else's inferiority.

Furthermore, as a result of this rationalization we lose our ability to act differently and to see that there is in fact something wrong with our actions. That is, our power and our perception of ourselves are weakened. In *Utopia* More describes pride as a "serpent from hell [which] entwines itself around the hearts of men and acts like the suckfish in preventing and hindering them from entering on a better way of life" (243/39–245/2).

Moreover, Thomas More does not think that this kind of psychological process is a rare phenomenon. If that were the case then he would not give so much attention to Utopia's institutions. He worries about protecting the entire citizenry from the vice. Thus, More seems to see all of us as having an ingrained predisposition to feelings of superiority. That is, "good" people become proud, and entire societies can be infected with the vice. That is why he is so concerned with institutions. Without the right institutions, whole societies are affected by pride.

Thomas More's understanding of the psychology of pride should probably be regarded as one of his most important accomplishments. Admittedly, More does not explore the inner world of the human psyche as profoundly as Augustine or Freud. However, More apparently hypothesized that the human personality is so constituted that exposure to a particular set of material conditions triggers a narcissism so powerful that it can literally alter one's perception of reality. And this notion undergirds the structure of Utopia's social, political, economic, and religious institutions.

By building his ideal society as much as he does on a particular understanding of the workings of the personality, Thomas More goes a step beyond the ancient philosophical tradition which links utopian speculation more to general theories of human nature or human happiness. This is still far short of Marx's understanding of the effect of material conditions on the human mind and the map of our inner mechanism drawn by psychologists like Freud and Jung, but More's contribution is still impressive in its own right.

NOTES

1. Richard C. Marius, *Thomas More: A Biography* (New York: Knopf, 1984), p. 153.

2. *The Meaning of More's* UTOPIA (Princeton: Princeton University Press, 1983), pp. 9–10.

3. Praising what he calls More's "systemic view of social problems," George Logan describes this as being "one of the most modern aspects of his book, anticipating not only the elaborate causal analysis that we expect from social planners but the understanding that solutions to social problems are to be sought in well-designed legal and institutional adjustments, not in moralistic condemnation of the consequences of the problems" (see above, p. 12).

4. As Logan explains elsewhere in this volume, "This, then, is the context in which Hythloday's account of Utopia is introduced: a dispute about the degree of compatibility of the moral and the expedient, and in particular whether the ideal of equality is compatible with stability and prosperity. This context suggests that the imaginary commonwealth constitutes some kind of *test* of the degree of compatibility of *honestas* and *utilitas*; that, whatever else it may be, it also constitutes an attempt to answer this fundamental theoretical question about the best condition of the commonwealth: Is it possible, even theoretically, for a commonwealth to be at once *prudentissima* and *sanctissima,* both shrewd and holy?" (p. 20).

5. See above, p. 32.

6. "In *Utopia*," he writes, "as later on, we find the Thomas More who saw the world as a wicked place and the human heart as a pit of darkness requiring the light of diligent public scrutiny if the monsters lurking there were not to crawl out and devour the person and the society. . . . More was to the marrow of his bones a medieval Christian, saturated with pessimism about a frail humankind weakened by original sin" (*Thomas More,* pp. 154, 167).

7. Ibid., pp. 167, 169.

8. *More's* UTOPIA: *The Biography of an Idea* (Princeton: Princeton University Press, 1952), p. 80.

9. Desiderius Erasmus to Ulrich von Hutten, in *Thomas More, 7 February 1477 – 6 July 1535: A Portrait in Words by His Friend Erasmus* [ed. John C. Olin] (New York: Fordham University Press, 1977),

p. 11; Peter Giles to Jerome Busleyden, in *Utopia,* edd. Edward Surtz, s.j., and J. H. Hexter, The Yale Edition of the Complete Works of St. Thomas More 4 (New Haven and London: Yale University Press, 1965), p. 23/11–14.

10. "Omnium princeps parensque pestium superbia" (p. 242/25–26).

11. Ed. W. E. Campbell, The English Works of Sir Thomas More 1 (London: Eyre & Spottiswoode, 1931), p. 477.

12. Ed. Garry E. Haupt, The Yale Edition of the Complete Works of St. Thomas More 13 (New Haven and London: Yale University Press, 1976), pp. 3/25, 64/26.

13. *Four Last Things,* p. 477.

14. Ibid.

15. Ibid.

16. P. 9/28.

17. Edd. Louis L. Martz and Frank Manley, The Yale Edition of the Complete Works of St. Thomas More 12 (New Haven and London: Yale University Press, 1976), p. 158/7–8.

18. "To Gonell," in *St. Thomas More: Selected Letters*, ed. Elizabeth Frances Rogers (New Haven and London: Yale University Press, 1961), p. 106; *Four Last Things*, p. 478; *Dialogue of Comfort*, pp. 158/12, 161/3.

19. It is important to note that Book I and Raphael's peroration on pride were written at roughly the same time. (On the composition of *Utopia,* see, of course, Hexter, *Biography of an Idea*.) This makes it plausible to assert that Thomas More had in mind the harm pride was working in the world around him as he wrote the dialogue of council and the scene at Morton's court.

20. Morton's attitude that Hythloday's remarks are worth considering stands out, of course, in stark contrast to the narrowmindedness of those around him. But Morton is not the king, so his approval of Raphael's idea does not guarantee that the philosopher's advice will even be seriously considered, much less actually tried. Also, it must not be overlooked that even this laudable councilor has apparently surrounded himself with sycophants. Morton's response does not overturn Raphael's claim that the common good is not the primary concern of centers of power.

21. The councilors whom Hythloday excoriates are, of course,

simply a foil for an attack against the monarchs whose pride drives the madness of their underlings. (But More could hardly risk such a direct attack—especially as he is seeking entry into the royal service.) No one in the realm would match the king in terms of wealth, power, and the dangerous sense of superiority which More believed would probably result.

22. P. 477.

4

Utopia and Martyrdom

GERMAIN MARC'HADOUR
Université Catholique de l'Ouest

SEVERAL CONSIDERATIONS have prompted me to tackle a
most implausible theme by seeking the folly of martyrdom
in that "praise of wisdom" called *Utopia*.

The world and the Church commemorated in 1985, not
the lives, but the deaths, of John Fisher and Thomas More.
The first celebration of the Amici Thomae Mori in that
year was a jubilee pilgrimage to Rome, coinciding to the
day with the fiftieth anniversary of their canonization on
May 19, 1935.[1] This supreme accolade was given them by
Pope Pius XI on the sole ground of their having shed their
blood in the cause of Christ. Considered in all its circumstances, such a way of dying was considered miracle
enough.[2]

My second reason for treating this topic is its *topicality*:
we live in an age of martyrs. More people have witnessed
to their faith with their lives in the last fifty years than
during any one century of mankind's past, including the
bloody convulsive ages of the Reformation and the French
Revolution. In 1935 the Holy See raised Fisher and More
to the altars as models of resistance to dictators "even unto
death," and their example did inspire many victims of overt
or covert persecution.

The Miracle of Martyrdom

The term "martyr," even though it has broadened its meaning and in the process shed much of its original acceptation—the Greek μάρτυς signifies "witness"[3]—is so closely associated with its New Testament matrix that its only occurrence in *Utopia* is linked to the first preaching of the Christian faith in the Isle. The whole sentence in which the word appears deserves close rereading. Describing "the religions of the Utopians" in the last and longest section of his account, the narrator Raphael Hythloday finds in them a superstitious distrust of any "change of religions," which means that they are not the stuff of which converts are made. "And yet," he continues, "after they had received from us the name of Christ, His teaching, His character, His miracles, and the no less miraculous constancy of so many martyrs, whose blood freely shed has drawn such populous nations far and near into His fellowship, you would not believe how readily disposed they were to join it."[4] The point is that martyrdom, at least on a large scale, is a miracle; it transcends human nature and therefore attests a supernatural power at work. The unusual, "incredible" courage of an isolated individual can always be credited to that one person's being a "superman," and need not be read as the seal of God, as a clear sign of God's presence. The New Testament already refers to "such a cloud of witnesses surrounding us."[5] Numbers matter. "One man is no man," even where martyrs are concerned.[6]

What Do Utopians Witness To?

If they were impressed by Christ's miracles, though they had familiar experience of miracles in their own midst,[7] the

Utopians found a specific challenge in a phenomenon they had presumably never encountered: the willingness to seal one's faith with one's death. Their own religion was not a faith proper. Even if their God was a loving parent, he had not spoken to them directly. His word was only his likeness printed in their "nature and reason" and an inclination in their hearts, but not an explicit revelation. And yet the majority of them witness to his love and justice by looking forward eagerly to an afterlife of his providing. And a considerable number of Utopians, nicknamed *Buthrescae,* that is, "mightily religious," rise to heroism by living *sub specie aeternitatis.* Whereas the bulk of the community bestow their leisure, of which there is plenty, on the bettering of their minds (p. 35/20) and on "the contemplation of nature" (p. 224/19), "there are some, however—nor are they few by any means—who, prompted by religion, neglect learning, show no concern to acquire knowledge, and never take a leave from work, their only purpose being to merit future, posthumous happiness by keeping themselves busy with good services to all the others."[8]

This startling passage has not received enough attention, considering that religion is central to the Utopian commonwealth and that the *Buthrescae,*[9] far from being a fringe group, are the veins of the social body. Paradoxically, like true disciples of Christ, they are "in the world without being of the world" (Jn 17:15–16). Moreover, odd though they are, they are not marginal; indeed they are indispensable. Like all saints, they become different and singular by pushing to the extreme the otherworldly spirit by which their fellow-citizens are also assumed to behave, and to an exemplary degree do behave (pp. 166/2f., 178/4). By forfeiting the leisure needed for "the freedom and culture of the mind," they renounce that which is the prime goal of their nation's policy (p. 135/20). Such Utopians as choose to work extra hours at their respective crafts simply because they are not inclined to contemplation oblige the community while following their own bent (p. 128/9–12); they are not witnesses to anything except the variety of humors in mankind. The *Buthrescae* go much further and obey loftier motives. The hard and dirty tasks for which they volunteer would hardly appeal to anybody, let alone to a considerable group. They serve the sick, clean cesspools, mend bridges, dig turf and sand and stones, fell and chop up trees, do the heavy carting; in a word, they make themselves the slaves, or worse than slaves, of all potential masters, public or private. Through their unremitting labor, they provide everyone else with the commodity most desired in Utopia: *otium,* free time for a liberal education and a contemplative life. And where they come nearest to the Christian ideal is in performing these chores "gladly and cheerfully"—*libentes hilaresque* (p. 224/31). Nor are they prompted by any pharisaic leaven of a "holier than thou" attitude. They "claim no credit; they neither chide the life of others nor extol their own" (p. 224/32–33). They are not a self-conscious elite. Yet the more they make their service available, the greater the honor they receive from all (p. 226/1).

Oddest of the *Buthrescae* are a body of celibates, who, like More's Carthusian neighbors and sometime hosts, are also vegetarians. At antipodic variance with Utopia's Epicurean philosophy, they reject all the pleasures of this life as harmful—*tanquam noxijs* (p. 226/4)—and gape only after the future life, the hope of which invigorates and exhilarates them. We are not told whether this group is large, and we get the impression that it includes no women. Nor do we learn anything about the family life of the *Buthrescae* who engage in wedlock; they avoid only such pleasures as

hinder their service and they welcome meat because it in-
creases their fitness.

Raphael ends his longish report on these "religious" with
an intriguing remark: the Utopians hold the married ones
to be "more prudent" or "wiser," and the celibates to be
"more saintly" or "holier"—*Hos Vtopiani prudentiores, at illo
sanctiores reputant* (p. 226/11–12). These epithets are not so
transparent as they may look. Their full weight can best
be assessed by examining the two or three dozen places in
Utopia where "prudence" and "sanctity" are mentioned,
especially the two sentences in which they are coupled. The
first, which also includes the verb *reputo—quum apud ani-
mum meum reputo prudentissima atque sanctissima instituta Vto-
piensiam* (p. 102/27)—in Father Surtz's English rendering,
"when in my heart I ponder on the extremely wise and
holy institutions of the Utopians" (p. 103/32), does less
than full justice to the double superlative and makes nothing
of the mild adversative *atque*. One might, without excessive
paraphrasing, say: "institutions which are most prudent
and at the same time most holy."[10] The second joint use of
the two words concerns euthanasia. To choose death when
life is an incurable torture is "to do wisely"—*prudenter*—
and doing so "by the counsels of the priests, who are God's
interpreters," makes the deed also "pious and holy"—*pie
sancteque* (p. 186/14–16). In all these contexts, natural reason is distinguished from, yet coupled with, the prompt-
ings of religion.

One might wince at hearing me say that the *Buthrescae*
"*gape* after the life to come." In Father Surtz's version, they
"long for it," but Paul Turner wisely points out the pejorative undertone of *inhiant* (p. 226/6).[11] The verb *inhiare*
means "to stare at something with one's mouth open." He
also anglicizes *Buthrescae* as "Cowparsons" to render the

element of monstrous exaggeration he sees conveyed by the prefix βου-.[12] Turner's remarks have the virtue of making us wonder whether More shares the enthusiasm of Hythloday for the godsend of godly citizens who solve the problem of the city's dirty work, a major headache for other designers of happy commonwealths. More cannot but like these edifying creatures of his, but he may well view their single-mindedness in a humorous light, as Erasmus makes Dame Folly expose the "sweet madness" of grammarians and "fanatic" scholars.[13] In an island which rates oxen far above horses on four different counts (p. 115), the bovine prefix may have warm overtones. Yet the doggedness of Buthrescan devotion does seem to be a near-caricature. Would More, who taught his family to tend the aged and the sick, have wished for any of his children to become a *Buthresca*? He himself contemplated joining the Order of Friars Minor. Now, St. Francis' charitable commitment to Assisi's lepers began with a kiss. This gesture might symbolize what is lacking in Utopia, even among the most serviceable citizens. They will do things for you and bear your burden, but do they ever stop to listen or to talk, beyond receiving your orders? They offer free charring galore, but rather little *charitas*. If I can pursue my punning, the *Buthrescae,* so agape for a reward, are but little concerned with *agapè*. They out-Martha Martha and have no share in Mary's "better part," praised at the end of Erasmus' *Moria*[14] and in various works of More's, whether he is asserting the price of contemplation, warning himself and his readers against the maelstrom of "busyness," or defending "blessed Mary Maudlin" against the rabid prophets of a social Gospel.[15]

The archetype of Christian service was familiar to More's public through the liturgy of Holy Thursday, called

Maundy after the Latin antiphon *"Mandatum novum do vobis,"* which More translates "I give you a new commandment, that ye love together [one another] as I have loved you."[16] The scene of Jesus' washing his disciples' feet and the order he gives them to wash each other's feet (Jn 13:14) beatify the rendering of menial service by putting it in a family atmosphere, in the context of a festive banquet. Jesus has "risen from supper" to play the ritual of humble service, and He "sits down again" for a long vigil during which heart freely speaks to heart. John's lying on the Master's breast (Jn 13:25) expresses well the intimacy of this complex relationship and the human affection that tempers the religious awe, the incarnate God being also friend and brother.[17] Like the Jewish scribe of Mk 12:34, the *Buthrescae* "are not far from the kingdom of God"; like him, though, they will get a perceptible boost if and when they receive the spirit of Christ. They live by the wisdom of the Old Testament, which tells us to watch the ant and learn from it (Pr 6:6), whereas Jesus wants us to learn from the birds of the air (Mt 6:26).

BONDSMAN TO KNIGHT

To enrich this *explication de texte* with another parameter, one can draw on the ideal of chivalry, which was dear to More's heart.[18] The feudal bond, mainly economic between landlord and villain, was essentially personal along the line from page through squire and knight to captain and king. The self-serving element in the devotion of the *Buthrescae* is what makes it antipodic to Christian chivalry. Their "alacrity born of hope"—*spe alacres* (p. 226/6)—may at first sight resemble the theological virtue of hope, but its roots, and therefore its fruits, are quite different. St. Paul's *spe gaudentes,* "merry in hope," is inseparable from the next two words, *Domino servientes* (Rm 12:12), and More couples the two when in prison he urges his family "to serve God and be merry and rejoice in him."[19] More rebukes the Lutheran Johann Bugenhagen for teaching that a virtuous deed is totally marred if the doer had an eye for reward.[20] He defends the value of merit and reward. Yet, following Pico, he lists gratuitous service among the properties of a lover.[21] And he prays: "Give me, good Lord, a longing to be with thee, not . . . so much for the attaining of the joys of heaven in respect of mine own commodity, as even for a very love to thee."[22] If he "sets at right nought" the loss of "life and all," it is "for the winning of Christ."[23] What the *Buthrescae* strive for, and truly bargain for, is "a maximum of happiness in a future life" (p. 226/5). This reaching beyond the horizon of the earth makes them a different race from the proles or Calibans conditioned to perform, and sometimes enjoy, menial tasks in some futuristic utopias. They have greater kinship with some Christian socialists of the nineteenth century. Anna Lee's Shakers, as described by Patrick Dooley in *Thought* and in *Moreana,* seem to me the nearest actualization of More's *Buthrescae.*[24] They yearned for the Second Coming of Christ, and in that vivid perspective "work was not a curse but a sacrament." Long hours of hard work were, of course, a sacrifice, but one made gladly on the altar of religion.

Buthrescan avidity to touch the heavenly dividends of their earthly investments reaches an almost suicidal level, insofar as they count on "their watching and sweat" to shorten their time of serving and waiting (p. 226/5–6). For the Christian, all the way to heaven partakes of heaven, even though a longing develops "to be out of this world" for a fuller enjoyment of God and Christ.[25]

The full flowering of grace is not so much bliss as glory, a biblical term which has colored the knightly concept of honor. The militant Christian reckons on "a weight of glory" (1 Co 1:17) as his due share in the triumph of his liege lord. The path of discipleship is through a cross to a crown, neither of which has a place in Utopia. This does not mean that More disapproves of Utopia's religion, which is a reasonable and yet warm theism. He himself advises the rich to "buy heaven" through almsdeeds, as Christ already urges the children of light to be as shrewd in the business of securing their eternal salvation as the children of this world are in the pursuit of their interests.

One final remark: the self-centeredness of the *Buthrescae,* even while they seem to sacrifice themselves for the welfare of others, appears also in the fact that they have *chosen* that way of life. Conversely, the Christian is attentive to heaven's call, and sees the initiative as belonging to God. This applies eminently to martyrdom, and is one more reason for not at all granting the *Buthrescae* the title of martyrs. The adverb *sponte* in *sponte fusus sanguis* (quoted in note 4) may give the impression that Christian martyrs can shed their blood of their own accord, and by choice. The spontaneity of some early martyrs may have led Raphael to use the word, but More in his prison meditation shows the limits of this self-exposure to death: it is a virtue only "when the case clearly demands it, or when God gives a secret prompting to do so."[26]

To deflate the pride of a monk, a little too conscious of having chosen the better part, contemplation, More warns him against self-delusion. By entering the cloister, he writes, you may have been dodging the demands of the normal human existence.[27] The Buthrescan choice of *vita activa*[28] at the expense of contemplation may equally well be an *alibi,* the seeking of a refuge in constant activity from having to face oneself.

More's Utopians "are easy-going . . . and leisure-loving"—*gens facilis . . . ocio gaudens* (p. 178/30–31). The honor they bestow on their voluntary slaves (p. 226/1) may resemble the cynical consideration reserved by the rulers of *Animal Farm* for the horse who toils and moils to the breaking of his back. Applause is given, but not that highest homage which is imitation. If the comfort they afford is sincerely appreciated, their persons are hardly admired; nor does their long-term investment create much interest, or arouse envy and emulation.

The word μάρτυς assumed the meaning of "witness par excellence," "witness with one's life," in the very first decades of the Church's history. It has probably entered the vocabulary of the Utopian language with the recording of those "many martyrs" whose cumulative testimony has prepossessed the *anima naturaliter christiana* of not a few Utopians. And inevitably the word will apply to some of them who have embraced Christianity. Persecution is inevitable for "all who are determined to live a holy life in Christ" (2 Tm 3:12). The risk of it is greater here because the Utopians' common denominator in religion is more of an ideology, and far less of a faith, than the Gospel just sprung on them by the Portuguese sailors. There is little of the genuine martyr in the neophyte exiled for his assault on all other religions; he suffers for preaching Christ "with more zeal than prudence—*maiore studio quam prudentia* (p. 218/22). But real persecution can be predicted of the kind that sent hundreds of Christians, mostly women, to their deaths in eighteenth-century Korea for breaking free of the social and patriarchal corset. The Land of the Morning Calm, cordoned off from the whole world, rather resembled More's Isle of Nowhere. Total isolation led their first Christian community to carry out a plan which at Hythloday's departure the budding church of Utopia was debating: to secure the sacraments by electing one from its own ranks and ordaining him priest.[29]

This debate within the Church at Amaurotum seems not to have been divisive. It hints, however, at a solution: namely, the arrival of some clergyman ordained by the pope or a bishop, which is sure to alienate the Christians from a self-contained society where offices at all levels are filled by election. Other confrontations are in store, since their faith will make them less permissive than the law on divorce and euthanasia allows and more indulgent toward adultery than the national ethos. One Christian among them has been banished for the manner of his teaching; others are bound to be taken to task and punished for the content of their belief. Christ's wisdom, "a folly unto the Greeks" (1 Co 1:18–23), will very soon appear alarmingly foolish to More's Austral Grecians. The Christians' confessing their sins to foreign priests outside the household will cause umbrage to the more autocratic patriarchs. Some young women are sure to outrage their parents by refusing to marry and be mothers. Other forms of unreasonableness will threaten the logic that holds Utopia together and will fissure the safe monolith. The cross of Christ will prove anathema to these husbanders of man's pleasure instinct. And yet, one may hope that a land of tolerance and of piety will be more receptive than most nations to the Gospel. The prayer that climaxes the public liturgy of Utopia is one the Christians can continue to recite with their fellow-citizens as an heroic testimony to God's all-sufficiency. Because Raphael Hythloday is so confident that such a perfect commonwealth will never change, we forget that the Uto-

71

pians themselves are ready to change if heaven invites them to do so. My conclusion will be a paraphrase, in direct style, of what every worshiper is supposed to say:

> You are the creator and ruler of the universe, the source of all that is good. I give you thanks for all your benefits, and especially for two blessings: inheriting a society which is the best of all and a religion that I hope is the truest of all. If I am wrong, and if something exists which is better than either, I beg your goodness to give me knowledge of it, and I am prepared to follow wherever you lead.[30]

Clearly they trust their political system more than their religion. The discipline imposed by King Utopus has been a *praeparatio evangelica,* and we can dream—Utopia entails some dreaming—that the nation will graduate into the Gospel, if not without debate and friction and some banishment, at least without bloodshed.

NOTES

1. These jubilee events—literally hundreds of them—are for the most part echoed, when not fully covered, in *Moreana.*

2. Two miracles are a normal prerequisite for canonization. If Fisher and More were exempted, it was not for the sheer fact that they died "for the faith of the Catholic Church," but for the style, the quality, of their witnessing through the long ordeal which began even before their incarceration: their patience, their serenity (and even joy at the end), their prayerful love of those who sought their blood showed them as true followers of Christ, "filled with grace and the Holy Spirit."

3. Like other Greek words adopted by early Christian writers, "martyr" took on a specific connotation, and in the Book of Revelation, which has been analyzed as "an open letter to the martyrs," it begins to designate those witnesses par excellence who lay down their lives for the living God who had conquered them by laying

down His life for their ransom. The semantic threshold is crossed in Rv 17:6 where the Whore of Babylon is shown "drunk with the blood τῶν μαρτύρων," a word that the Vulgate transliterates as *martyrum* instead of *testium*.

4. "At posteaquam acceperunt a nobis CHRISTI nomen, doctrinam, mores, miracula, nec minus mirandam tot martyrum constantiam, quorum sponte fusus sanguis, tam numerosas gentes in suam sectam longe lateque traduxit, non credas quam pronis in eam affectibus etiam ipsi concesserint . . ." (*Utopia,* edd. Edward Surtz, s.j., and J. H. Hexter, The Yale Edition of the Complete Works of St. Thomas More 4 [New Haven and London: Yale University Press, 1965], pp. 216/32–218/2). All further references in my text are to the page and line numbers of this edition. Though I have relied on it for the Latin text, the English translations are, unless otherwise indicated, my own. In the English sentence, Father Surtz failed to retain the play on *miracula/mirandum.* My "miracle . . . miraculous" comes from Paul Turner's version of *Utopia* (Harmondsworth: Penguin, 1965), p. 118.

5. Heb 12:1: τοσοῦτον ἔχοντες περικείμενον ἡμῖν νέφος μαρτύρων. The Vulgate has kept the "cloud" metaphor: *tantam habentes impositam nubem testium.* And so has Erasmus in his New Testament: *quum tanta septi simus nube testium.*

6. In Erasmus' dialogue about Pope Julius II's being "excluded from heaven," the *Julius Exclusus,* written only two years before *Utopia,* St. Peter reminds his warlike successor that the Church is spread by "the blood of martyrs and ours." Martyrdom is an ongoing, essential dimension of Christian discipleship. See the reference (*Utopia,* edd. Surtz and Hexter, p. 519) in the note commenting on p. 216/34. Writing from prison to his sister Elizabeth about "The Ways to Perfect Religion," John Fisher stirs her devotion to "the sweet Jesu" by evoking the "martyrs innumerable both men and women [who] for his love have shed their blood" (*The English Works of John Fisher,* ed. John E. B. Mayor [London: Early English Text Society, 1876], p. 384).

7. Miracles "witnessing the deity's presence" in the world of men occur "frequently" in Utopia, and are confidently sought in all public emergencies (p. 224/15ff.). They testify that God cares. They are tokens of His parental providence. When performed by Christ

or His disciples, a miracle can also be a sign, which attests that God
is with them, authenticating their message.

8. "Sunt tamen, hijque haud sane pauci, qui religione ducti, li-
teras negligunt, nulli rerum cognitioni student, neque ocio prorsus
ulli uacant, negocijs tantum, bonisque in caeteris officijs statuunt,
futuram post fata felicitatem promereri" (p. 224/20–24).

9. I apply the label to the whole group just described. It occurs,
however, only at the end of Hythloday's account of these "religious"
(p. 226/17) after a *Huiusmodi* that may designate only the more ascetic "school."

10. Or "which are both extremely sensible and extremely holy."

11. Turner, in his *Utopia,* p. 145*n*41, avoids the pejorative connotation by translating *inhiant* as "yearn for." G. C. Richards in his
translation (*Utopia* [Oxford: Oxford University Press, 1923]) says
the Buthrescans "set upon the hope" of heaven. The word *inhiant*
occurs only once in the Latin Bible, to characterize "bloodthirsty
enemies" of the Jews—*Hostes eorum inhiabant sanguini* (Est 9:1). The
Douay version renders it as "gaped after their blood." St. Augustine
uses *inhianter* to qualify young Monica's craving for libations of wine
(*Confessions* 9.8.18).

To the objection that More, himself an ascetic, could hardly wish
to ridicule a behavior simply because it defies common sense, Turner
answers that More "was quite capable of seeing his own actions in
a humorous light" (*Utopia,* p. 145).

12. The epicene *Buthrescae,* and even the masculine *religiosi* that
translates it, do not exclude women. One cannot tell "s'il s'agit
d'hommes, ou de femmes," as André Prévost says in the note on
célibataires in his *L'Utopie de Thomas More* (Paris: Mame, 1978),
p. 603. Yet his own "des hommes" (p. 602) creates an assumption
of maleness, as does the triple *men* of Robert Adams, especially the
third one—"religious men"—in his translation of *Utopia* (New
York: Norton, 1975), p. 83. Paul Turner's bias is even more explicit
when he anglicizes *Buthrescae* as "Cowparsons" and *religiosi* as "Lay
Brethren" (*Utopia,* p. 123). Ralph Robynson already was so steeped
in this reading that he translated *Venere . . . abstinent* by "abstaining
. . . from the company of women" (*Utopia,* ed. J. H. Lupton [Ox-
ford: Clarendon, 1895], p. 281). One would hesitate, admittedly, to
wish any woman the company of such an intense group of eager
beavers.

13. *The Praise of Folly,* trans. Clarence H. Miller (New Haven and London: Yale University Press, 1979), pp. 79f. The wise fools include, of course, those who write books.

14. Ibid., p. 137, with reference to Lk 10:38–42.

15. To the five different works of More's listed in my *The Bible in the Works of St. Thomas More* II (Nieuwkoop: De Graaf, 1969), p. 110, add his *Life of John Picus* (*The English Works of St. Thomas More* [London, 1557]), p. 14D.

16. Jn 13:34, as quoted in *A Dialogue Concerning Heresies,* edd. Thomas M. C. Lawler, Germain Marc'hadour, and Richard C. Marius, The Yale Edition of the Complete Works of St. Thomas More 6 (New Haven and London: Yale University Press, 1981), p. 107/16.

17. Though "the whole island is like one family" (p. 148/3), the solidarity is not expressed as brotherly love, one more reason for questioning Turner's term "Lay Brethren." The word *frater* occurs but once in Book II of *Utopia,* in the chapter on war, where we see the Utopians' attempt to destabilize an enemy kingdom "by leading a brother of the king . . . to hope that he may obtain the throne" (p. 205/34–35). True, the *frater* of Book I (pp. 82–84) is a rather unbrotherly friar who makes us fear an overdose of fraternity.

18. See my "Sir Thomas More, Knight," *Catholic Theological Review,* 2 (1979), 3–19.

19. *The Correspondence of Sir Thomas More,* ed. Elizabeth F. Rogers (Princeton: Princeton University Press, 1947), p. 532/671. The phrase "merry in God" (ibid., pp. 544/165 and 432/39) also echoes Ph 4:4.

20. Ibid., p. 353/1046–49.

21. *English Works of St. Thomas More,* pp. 27D and 32A: "For very love, without any regard / To any profit. . . ."

22. "A Devout Prayer," in *A Treatise on the Passion,* ed. Garry E. Haupt, The Yale Edition of the Complete Works of St. Thomas More 13 (New Haven and London: Yale University Press, 1976), p. 230/7.

23. Ibid., p. 227/14–16.

24. "More's *Utopia* and the New World," *Thought,* 60, No. 1 (March 1985), 31–48; briefly revisited as "Theory in *Utopia* vs. Practice in Utopias," *Moreana,* 87–88 (November 1986), 57–60.

25. Over the years More expresses this longing with increasing frequency, using the proverbial *Cupio dissolvi*. See my *The Bible in the Works of St. Thomas More* III (Nieuwkoop: De Graaf, 1970), under Ph 1:23, pp. 113–14.

26. The vocation to martyrdom is examined at some length in *De tristitia Christi*, ed. Clarence H. Miller, The Yale Edition of the Complete Works of St. Thomas More 14 (New Haven and London: Yale University Press, 1976). I have quoted from Miller's "The Heart of the Final Struggle" in *Quincentennial Essays on St. Thomas More*, ed. Michael Moore (Boone, N.C., 1978), p. 118. Of himself, while he tries to ward off the final blow, More says: "I put not myself forward, but draw back" (*Correspondence of Sir Thomas More,* ed. Rogers, p. 559/132).

27. *Correspondence of Sir Thomas More,* ed. Rogers, pp. 190–91, and more specifically p. 203/1449f.: "timereque tecum, ne tu vel in Mariae parte non sis, vel Mariae partem perperam delegeris. . . ."

28. Addiction to work to the extent of leaving no room for contemplation is, apparently, what is suggested by the gloss *Vita activa* (p. 224/22), which serves as a section-title.

29. See Germain Marc'hadour and Henry Gibaud, "Election ou ordination? Tentation utopienne et tentative coréenne," *Moreana,* 87–88 (1985), 167–71.

30. "In his deum & creationis, & gubernationis, & caeterorum praeterea bonorum omnium, quilibet recognoscit autorem, tot ob recepta beneficia gratias agit, nominatim uero quod deo propitio in eam rempublicam inciderit quae sit felicissima, eam religionem sortitus sit, quam speret esse uerissimam. Qua in re, si quid erret, aut si quid sit alterutra melius, & quod deus magis approbet, orare se eius bonitas efficiat, hoc ut ipse cognoscat. paratum enim sequi se quaqua uersus ab eo ducatur . . ." (p. 236/12–19).

5

The Idea of Utopia
from Hesiod to John Paul II

JOHN C. OLIN
Fordham University

I INTEND in this essay to explore the idea of utopia. The
word is the invention of Thomas More's, and, as we know,
the title of his famous book. It comes from the Greek
οὐτόπος, which literally means "nowhere." In current
usage it signifies an ideal place or state, a perfect social
order or one nearly so. It carries overtones of something
visionary or imaginary. I want to examine the nature of
such a concept or vision and probe some of the ways in
which it has been formulated and historically expressed. In
that regard Thomas More's book holds central place. I
would also like to evaluate the idea and its relevance today.
I realize this is a large order. The term "utopia" encom-
passes a broad spectrum of attitudes, aspirations, and en-
deavors. It is closely related to certain myths and important
religious beliefs; it has a connection with theories of progress and evolution; it can be identified with radical social
and political movements. In a short essay one can hardly
expect to do justice to such a theme, but I shall try to
throw some light on the subject at least and say something
useful about the character and history of the utopian idea.

Let me begin with what I believe is a primary and fundamental aspect of utopian thought, perhaps its source: namely, its religious manifestation or dimension. A passage in an essay I recently read by the Swiss theologian Hans Urs von Balthasar comes to mind and can serve as an opening text.

> Creation sighs for perfection, and the divine Spirit also sighs for perfection out of the depths of the human heart and out of all the beings subject to decay. God, in power and powerlessness, is most profoundly interested in this perfection. Therefore the Christian also, with every bit of his Christianity as well as his humanity, is involved with an interest that is actually divine in the perfection of the world.[1]

This striking pronouncement, mystical yet earth-bound, comes at the end of a volume entitled *Convergences* the theme of which is the reconciliation of diverse elements in our experience within the framework of Christian dogma. In that context von Balthasar elevates—theologizes, so to speak—the worldly striving for utopia. Christian doctrine, he stresses, gives positive meaning to the world and man's exertions in it. The passage echoes in my mind the prayer of the Our Father: "Thy kingdom come. Thy will be done on earth as it is in heaven." The petition encapsulates, does it not, the yearning for perfection von Balthasar describes, that is, the desire for utopia?

St. Augustine, the great theologian of the early and medieval Church, does not appear to share this same perspective. "The perfection of the world" was not his urgent concern. His *City of God,* which is nearly always heralded as introducing or elaborating the idea of progress in history, treats history as a progressive development, but its goal or final end is beyond history. Augustine's vision is totally eschatological. In this world two mystical cities, the heavenly and the earthly, coexist and intermingle, but on the last day, the day of judgment, they will be separated and their consummation reached. The good, those of the heavenly city who are pilgrims in this world, will reign with God evermore; the wicked, members of the earthly city, will be condemned to everlasting punishment.[2] So bald a summary does not do justice to the richness and depth of Augustine's great work, but it is clear that he posits a celestial utopia, not an earthly one. He did not grapple with issues of social or political reform or envisage a better society here and now.

Von Balthasar's quotation conveys a different message, as does the theological perception that underlies and inspires it. We are confronting two different traditions, two very different emphases within the framework of Christian revelation. One can be called the Augustinian; the other (I shall explain this further), the Christian humanist. The exclusivity of these traditions or emphases should not be exaggerated. They are separate interpretations stemming out of the Christian message, but there is a connection between them. The Christian faith is both transcendent and immanent. Its teachings have social implications. The heavenly goal can, and invariably does, have great bearing on worldly behavior.

We see this double aspect, this sometimes confusing ambivalence, and this interplay historically reflected in biblical messianism and in the notion of the Millennium, two subjects of great importance closely related to our theme. The messianic prophecies of the Old Testament (like St. Augustine's *City of God*) embody a providential conception of history as a process moving toward a final end, the kingdom of God. They also often assume a more secular or political form, focusing on the role or the restoration of the kingdom of Israel which David had consolidated and ruled as the ideal king. The Book of Isaiah presents an impressive compendium of these prophetic oracles in which the agent of victory, the heir of David, the Messiah to come, is seen as bringing deliverance and salvation and inaugurating the reign of justice and peace. These Isaian prophecies conclude with a triumphant vision of a world renewed.

> Lo, I am about to create new heavens and a new earth.
> The things of the past shall not be remembered or come to mind.
> Instead, there shall always be rejoicing and happiness in what I create;
> For I create Jerusalem to be a joy and its people to be a delight;
> I will rejoice in Jerusalem and exult in my people.
> No longer shall the sound of weeping be heard there, or the sound of crying . . . [Is 65:17–19].

The utopian character of this great expectation and vision is obvious, and although it is an eschatological projection, it has nevertheless a temporal foundation and relevance. We find it repeated almost word for word in the Apocalypse, the last book of the New Testament.

> Then I saw new heavens and a new earth. The former heavens and the former earth had passed away, and the sea was no longer. I also saw a new Jerusalem, the holy city, coming down out of heaven from God, beautiful as a bride prepared to meet her husband. I heard a loud voice from the throne cry out: "This is God's dwelling among men. He shall dwell with them and they shall be his people and he shall be their God who is always with them. He shall wipe every tear from their eyes, and there shall be no more death or mourning, crying out or pain, for the former world has passed away" [Rv 21:1–4].

The twofold character and ambivalence of the Old Testament prophecies is repeated in the recognition of Jesus and His mission. He was called "the king of the Jews" and viewed by His disciples as the Messiah who had been prophesied. His kingdom, however, was not of this world (Jn 18:33–36; Ac 1:6–8). His messianic mission was not to be confused with the restoration of the Davidic kingdom. He announced the kingdom of God and spoke of it often but in an entirely different sense (Mt 4:17; Mk 1:14–15 and 4:11, 26–32; Lk 17:20–21). It was now at hand, like "scattered seed"; it involved individual acceptance and conversion; it meant personal reform and change (the Greek word is μετάνοια), not political revolution.

Among the early Christians, however, there arose the expectation of an imminent Second Coming of Jesus which would mark the end of time and usher in the reign of God with his saints. "What we await are new heavens and a new earth where, according to his promise, the justice of God will reside" (2 P 3:13). Like the Isaian vision this was an eschatological hope. Millenarianism is a part of this expectation. It is the belief that following the Second Coming Jesus will establish an earthly kingdom in which He will rule with the righteous for a thousand years, that is, a millennium. This conviction, based on a passage in the Apocalypse (Rv 20:4–6), generated over the centuries a variety of sects and movements, most of them heretical, who pursued the Millennium—their utopia—often in violent ways.[3] The classic examples are the furious but short-lived revolutionary movements of Thomas Muntzer and of John of Leyden in Germany during the Reformation. But the Gospel message has also been understood, and primarily so, as bearing the news of personal renewal and salvation. "If anyone is in Christ, he is a new creation. The old order has passed away; now all is new" (2 Co 5:17). The messianic hope, the utopian vision, is expressed here on an individual scale.

I have briefly touched on basic elements in the Judaeo-Christian religious tradition that have inspired and informed the modern historical perspective and specifically notions of progress and utopia. This theme has frequently been developed by scholars who have written on the subject.[4] Modern thought in this regard is seen as a secularization of religious beliefs that lie at the foundation of Western culture. "I shall attempt to show," Carl Becker wrote in his *The Heavenly City of the Eighteenth-Century Philosophers,* "that the *Philosophes* demolished the Heavenly City of St. Augustine only to rebuild it with more up-to-date materials."[5] The "up-to-dateness" refers, of course, to the assumptions of the eighteenth-century *philosophes.* The religious and the secular, however, should not be viewed as diametrically opposed or as unable to coexist. Both Judaism and Christianity are historical religions whose doctrines involve events in this world and whose teachings have important secular ramifications. I have already indicated this above. The transcendence of these faiths is not at odds with the immanence of their message. The Christian doctrine of the Incarnation—"And the Word was made flesh and dwelt among us"—in fact unites the two spheres, as do many other Christian beliefs. It is this unity that von Balthasar stresses. It occurs to me also that the famous passage in St. John's First Epistle (1 Jn 4:7–21) linking God's love for us with our love for one another— "if God has loved us so, we must have the same love for one another"—is a striking statement of this concurrence. It expresses quintessentially a theology of utopia.

There are also the antecedents and sources for utopia in

pagan antiquity. Plato's *Republic,* of course, is the classic archetype for subsequent depictions of the ideal society. Aside from that famous work there is the ancient myth of a paradisiacal Golden Age in times long past. The Greek poet Hesiod (ca. 700 B.C.) is one of the first to tell us of such an age when men "lived like gods, with hearts free from care and without part or lot in labor and sorrow."[6] He describes this epoch of a Golden Race as the first in a deteriorating cycle of five ages that are ever recurrent. This view of history as a repetitive cyclical process is characteristic of Greek and Roman thought and is in sharp contrast to the progressive Judaeo-Christian historical perspective we have been discussing. It finds expression in many places, notably in Plato's *Statesman* (269C–274D), where the cyclical pattern of human events is related to change and revolution in the natural cosmos, and in the *Republic* (546A–547A), where the ideal society Plato describes is equated with the Golden Age and the degeneration of the ruling Guardian class, a Golden Race, is seen as following a natural as well as a Hesiodic cycle. Vergil's fourth *Eclogue* (ca. 40 B.C.) has one of the most moving evocations of the cyclical view and of the return of the Golden Age:

> The last age of the Cumaean song now has come;
> The great order of the ages is born anew.
> Now the virgin returns, the reign of Saturn returns;
> Now a new offspring is sent down from heaven on high.
> Look with favor, chaste Lucina, on the child now being born.
> With him the iron race ends and a race of gold springs up
> Throughout the world. Now your Apollo rules.

The passage is replete with excitement and hope. The Golden Age is again at hand. There is little wonder that St. Augustine and others interpreted the *Eclogue* as a messianic prophecy foretelling the coming of Christ.

83

But the most explicit and extended statement of utopianism in antiquity is Plato's *Republic*. It is the most famous and influential of his dialogues. The work is a discussion, with Socrates the main spokesman, about the nature of justice, which is observed and examined in terms of the well-ordered state. In the projection of this ideal society, the role of the Guardians or ruling class is seen as all-important, and their education and way of life are described at length. They have no private possessions and live a completely communal life. Even their wives and children are held in common. The total communality among the Guardians is the keynote of the *Republic* and the reason for the order and harmony of the model state that is envisioned. Everyone else in the society under the enlightened government of the Guardians adheres unswervingly to his craft and class.

Plato (it is Socrates who speaks in the dialogue) acknowledges that he is presenting an ideal, a pattern of justice, not a model polity that can be realized as such (471C–473E). The one practical step toward good government that he does urge is that philosophers become kings or kings philosophers. Otherwise, so it would seem, his prescriptions are for personal inspiration and guidance. They are a standard for the virtuous life. An extremely interesting passage at the end of Book IX quite clearly bears this out. The discussion has come to a reference by Socrates to the city in which the wise man will dwell and take part. Glaucon, his interlocutor, says:

> You mean the city whose establishment we have described, the city whose home is in the ideal, for I think that it can be found nowhere on earth.
> Well, said I, perhaps there is a pattern of it laid up in heaven for him who wishes to contemplate it and so beholding to

constitute himself its citizen. But it makes no difference whether it exists now or ever will come into being. The politics of this city only will be his and of none other [592A, B].

The similarity and kinship between this Platonic (or Socratic) view and St. Augustine's notion of the heavenly city is striking. One might even relate it to the kingdom of God that Jesus announced. In each case the paradigmatic community is a heavenly one, and membership in it here and now is a matter of personal conversion and adherence.

Aristotle, however, understood Plato's *Republic* as presenting the best form for the constitution of a well-governed state, and in his *Politics* (Book II, chaps. 1–5) he vigorously refuted its central theme of the sharing of wives and property by the Guardians. His arguments against the excessive communality and total unity of Plato's model state read like an indictment of communist collectivism in our own time. The evils of society, he declares (1263B 11–12), are not due to the possession of private property but arise out of defects in human character. The question of an ideal social order is again brought back to the issue of individual moral behavior. Nevertheless the notion of a community based on common ownership and the sharing of goods is an ancient and persistently attractive ideal. Pythagoras (sixth century B.C.) is said to have founded a religious society that embraced this concept and to have been the author of a proverb epitomizing it: "Friends have all things in common." This proverb which both Plato and Aristotle as well as many others quote is the first in a great collection of proverbs, the *Adagia,* which Erasmus compiled and published in many editions in the early sixteenth century. He gave the dictum pride of place in his collection and discussed it at length, equating it with Christ's command that we love one another. "Nothing ever said by a pagan philosopher," Erasmus asserted, "is more in keeping with the mind of Christ."[7] We know from the Acts of the Apostles (2:42–45 and 4:32–37) that the early Christians followed this rule: "Those who believed shared all things in common; they would sell their property and goods, dividing everything on the basis of each one's need." Their *communitas,* as Erasmus emphasized, embodied Christ's *charitas.*

This linkage is also found in Thomas More's *Utopia.* The communal order of the non-Christian commonwealth which the voyager Raphael Hythloday describes in More's book is seen as harmonious with Christian teaching and practice. When the Utopians first heard of Christianity from Hythloday and his companions, many were led to accept the faith and were baptized. Hythloday explains this by saying: "I think that this factor, too, was of no small weight, that they had heard that His disciples' common way of life had been pleasing to Christ and that it is still in use among the truest societies of Christians" (219/5–8).[8] The last reference is to monastic communities who practice poverty and follow a communal life. More, like Erasmus, had joined classical and Christian themes, a union typical of the Renaissance. But the union here is especially significant from our point of view. The pagan and Christian, man's natural reason and Revelation, combine to envision a better world and to point the way toward its attainment.

But what precisely is More's purpose? How are we to interpret what Professor Logan has called this "deeply enigmatic" work? As I stated in the Preface, More has raised so many provocative issues in *Utopia* and readers and scholars have approached it from so many different backgrounds and points of view and understood it in so many different ways that discussion about it is practically inexhaustible. Terence's maxim "So many men, so many opinions" is fully borne out in this instance.[9] And the essays in this volume give witness to this truth.

I am not going to discuss More's *Utopia* at great length here. I have given my overall interpretation of the work in an essay, "Erasmus' *Adagia* and More's *Utopia*," that recently appeared in *Moreana*.[10] Let me briefly summarize it. I related the defense of common ownership and the description of the communal life of the Utopians which is made by Hythloday in More's book to the adage "Friends have all things in common" which Erasmus so prominently expounds in his *Adagia*. I claimed that the two humanists were presenting in different ways the same moral and religious ideal. *Utopia* obviously is the more dramatic and complex presentation. Its Book I is a critique of the ills and injustices in English and European society in More's time; its Book II is the description of the ideal commonwealth of Utopia where the vices that plague Christendom have in large part been eliminated. The whole account is an imaginative dialogue between More and the voyager Hythloday, who has been to the New World and has seen the model society he describes. The two Books were composed separately but are marvelously complementary. They analyze and reveal two contrasting social orders whose comparison cannot fail to heighten perception and vigorously stimulate thought about our human relations and the morality or lack thereof that governs them.

Many questions arise in connection with all this. The major one is whether More should be taken literally in his (actually it is Hythloday who speaks) advocacy of communism, not of Marxism, of course, nor of the Soviet system, but of a social order nevertheless where there is no private property and all possessions are held in common.

Is he offering a model for a new and revolutionary social order? Is he seriously presenting this model as an attainable goal? The answer, I think, has to be nuanced. More is talking not so much about radical social reform as about radical individual reform. It is the personal qualities and virtues of the Utopians that account for the exemplary character of their commonwealth. This is particularly true of their moral philosophy, which is discussed at length in Book II. Good people have made a good society. More's book is actually about the values men live by.

Plato's Republic exists in the ideal and "can be found nowhere on earth." So too the island of Utopia, as its name informs us. It is a pattern, a paradigm "laid up in heaven for him who wishes to contemplate it and so beholding to constitute himself its citizen." But such personal perception and commitment can lead to social change. That is the thrust of *Utopia,* as I understand it. The Utopians, for example, believed in a "natural fellowship" that taught them to help one another and to "relieve the poverty and misfortunes of others," and they put their belief into practice. What a lesson for the Europeans! In the context of his times More wrote a Christian-humanist manifesto animated by the spirit of renewal and reform. His book reflects the humanism of the Renaissance as well as the impact of the discovery of America. By the same token it is witness to an incisive perspective on the problems and needs of his day. Erasmus hit the nail on the head when he wrote that More "published *Utopia* to show what the causes of our civil problems are, having England which he knows and understands so well particularly in mind."[11]

I said earlier I would explain what I meant by the term "Christian humanist." I used it at the beginning of this essay to distinguish Hans Urs von Balthasar's approach from the Augustinian and to characterize the view that Christianity has social implications and can motivate and guide social action. This approach is based on the belief that the Gospel message—what Erasmus calls "the philosophy of Christ"—is in accord with human nature and restores and perfects it.[12] In the classical and Renaissance sense of the word, *humanitas* (whence comes our word humanism) finds its fulfillment in the Christian revelation.[13] Like the lifework of Erasmus, More's *Utopia* embodies this perception.

Where does all this leave us in terms of our initial inquiry into the nature of utopian thought? A few observations can be made at this point. The first is that utopia as we understand and use the word in its broad sense today has roots and important antecedents in both the Judaeo-Christian and the classical traditions. It seems deeply embedded in our historical consciousness. A second is that common ownership and a sharing of goods—"Friends have all things in common"—are generally prominent features of the ideal society that is envisaged. A third is that there is some ambiguity about the exact character or status of the utopia that is projected, that is, about the way in which it should be understood. Is it meant as a social model, as "the best form" of a community or state, or is it to be interpreted on a more personal level, as an inspiration or standard for the individual and not as a paradigm for society at large? A fourth and last observation is that Thomas More's *Utopia* is an epitome of the traditions and aspects of the utopian idea as it has come down historically and found expression in the broad context of More's own time.

I would like to dwell a moment on the third observation. There are three points I want to make. One is that the two different views or ways of understanding utopia that I referred to do not necessarily entail a radical opposition. They are not mutually exclusive. Their distinction is important, but the two perspectives are interrelated and have a reciprocal bearing. They are two sides of the same coin, so to speak. I have already indicated this above. Point number two is that the two views of utopia—the personal and the social—correspond, it seems to me, to the two conceptions of the kingdom of God—the otherworldly or eschatological and the worldly or temporal—that I spoke of earlier in this essay. I mean that interpreting utopia as a personal standard and moral ideal is comparable to seeing the kingdom of God as a heavenly community. It may indeed be present in a spiritual and personal sense among those who are its members here and now—"The reign of God is already in your midst" (Lk 17:21)[14]—but as a society in the full or literal meaning of the word (as St. Augustine understood it) it is transcendental or eschatological. By the same token, viewing utopia as a social model or ideal is very similar to understanding the kingdom of God as a society or polity to be established on earth. These two sets of views not only correspond but at times tend to merge. The implications of this are extremely interesting. My third point is that utopia as a social model or ideal is the more common interpretation of the idea. It is the view we generally meet with when the idea is discussed or when some movement inspired by a utopian program or goal is launched.

There are any number of examples from More's time to our own to illustrate these and other aspects of utopian thought. Two early ones come to mind. Not long after it was published (it first appeared in 1516), *Utopia* was an inspiration for Vasco de Quiroga, the Spanish bishop of Michoacán in New Spain (today Mexico), who established Indian communities based on the model in More's classic.

Here was a startling reversal of the setting and even the thrust of More's theme. The vision of an ideal social order came back to the New World from the Old. The Mexican historian Silvio Zavala writes:

> Thus, More's *Utopia* was to be transformed into a Magna Carta of Hispano-Indian society. The task of the European should not be to transport to America *his* values, in order there to reproduce the same tortured society from which the humanist was fleeing, but to avail himself of the unformed and tractable mass of Indian population in order to produce from it the perfect Christian commonwealth.[15]

Quiroga's experiment was the first of a long series of efforts to establish utopian-type communities, a series particularly notable and rich in variety in the nineteenth century. An ardent religious ideal had also motivated Quiroga, who like so many of his Franciscan compatriots saw in the New World an opportunity for restoring the apostolic spirit and ways of the early Church. And for some it seemed that the time of the Millennial kingdom had also at long last arrived.[16] The Age of Discovery and its impact gave rise to utopian dreams on both sides of the Atlantic.

It was not all a dream, however. Contemporary with Quiroga's Indian experiment in Mexico Calvin sought to establish a Holy Commonwealth in Protestant Geneva, the actuality of which has been compared with More's Utopia. In an essay written several years ago, J. H. Hexter stressed the similarity in spirit and in many details between the two model societies and saw Christian humanism and the concomitant religious revival as their common matrix.[17] Calvin's zeal for moral and social reform flowed directly from his dynamic theology, but his concept and achievement have their parallel nevertheless in More's more secular vision. The Church doctrine and discipline that were the underpinnings of Calvin's theocratic community are the counterpart of the natural moral philosophy that inspired the Utopians. Conversion and conviction in both cases were the essential basic component. This linking of Calvin and More, of Geneva and Utopia, is revealing. Not only does it tell us something about the utopian idea per se, but it casts light on its attempted realization and the problems involved, that is, on the ideal as a social experiment as distinguished from mere discussion or speculation about it.

These Renaissance–Reformation reforms of the social order introduce us to the modern era of conscious social change and revolution. More and his immediate successors are its pioneers. Utopia in practice as well as in theory now became a viable and realistic goal. In this development the eighteenth century, the Age of Enlightenment, as it is called, was a decisive period. The Christian historical perspective, to follow Becker's thesis, was thoroughly secularized.[18] The universal laws of nature were seen as ensuring and effecting man's progress and perfectibility. Carl Becker writes:

> The utopian dream of perfection, that necessary compensation for the limitations and frustrations of the present state, having long been identified with the golden age or the Garden of Eden or life eternal in the Heavenly City of God, and then by the sophisticated transferred to remote or imagined lands (the moon or Atlantis or Nowhere, Tahiti or Pennsylvania or Peking), was at last projected into the life of man on earth and identified with the desired and hoped-for regeneration of society.[19]

Condorcet, as he awaited the guillotine in 1793, ironically gave us one of the most comprehensive transformations, *The Progress of the Human Mind.* It was a true act of faith

92

in the Age of Reason and the beneficence of history. He perceived mankind developing through ten historical stages to perfection, that is, to the ultimate utopia, Elysium in this world. "Nature has set no limit," he wrote, "to the realization of our hopes." Condorcet's theory of progress and view of history found fuller philosophical elaboration as well as greater historical impact with Hegel and Marx in the nineteenth century. Hegel's concept of the historical process was far more metaphysical, but it envisaged a purposeful, if somewhat abstruse, movement toward a final utopian goal. Marx rejected Hegel's mystical idealism but retained his notion of a dialectical historical process and gave it greater specificity and relevance. Unlike Hegel he was a materialist and an economic determinist. He saw history evolving through class struggle inevitably toward a classless society where justice and harmony and happiness would at last prevail, that is, toward utopia, toward the kingdom. Like Hythloday he denounced private property and focused on radical social change, and his interpretation of history both explained and guaranteed it. And like More's *Utopia* Marx's communism epitomized many of the dominant currents and aspirations in its time. Indeed it gave those currents and aspirations great coherence and dynamic power.

But alas, some fears and anxieties did arise. In his idiom William Butler Yeats sounded an early alarm:

> Surely some revelation is at hand;
> Surely the Second Coming is at hand;
> The Second Coming! Hardly are those words out
> When a vast image out of *Spiritus Mundi*
> Troubles my sight. . . .[20]

More than one vast image appeared in the twentieth century to put an end to utopianism, or at least seriously to question and challenge such suppositions. Erich Fromm in an Afterword to George Orwell's *1984* wrote that the First World War "was the beginning of that development which tended in a relatively short time to destroy a two-thousand-year-old Western tradition of hope and to transform it into a mood of despair."[21] Other horrendous events soon followed: Stalin, Hitler, the Second World War, nuclear weapons, Mao, Pol Pot, etc., etc. The old idea of progress and man's perfectibility echoed now like a cruel deception, a kind of Orwellian "doublethink." Gertrude Himmelfarb in a superb essay on the idea of progress calmly understates the case when she writes: "The experiences of this century hardly dispose us to any complacency about the present, still less about the future."[22] Thus anti-utopia or dystopia (from the Greek δυστόπος, meaning "bad place") entered our ken. Aldous Huxley's *Brave New World* and the more terrifying *1984* are two of its most haunting representations.

Is every idea of utopia now at an end? What lesson can we draw from its checkered history? Answers are not easily given. The present can be read in very different ways, depending on one's vantage point and cultural preconceptions, and the future, of course, is veiled. Modern science does seem to open up new possibilities—and bestow new powers—but the behavior of man is crucial, and science is not a guide to virtue or a guarantee of moral rectitude. Thomas More's comment that " 'it is impossible that all should be well unless all men were good' " (101/2–3) is still the irreducible bottom line.[23] Moral development or evolution in this regard is conceivable. Indeed the great Jesuit palaeontologist Teilhard de Chardin, whom Governor Cuomo quoted so perceptively in his opening remarks, has envisaged it, but, despite the plausibility of the Teilhardian conception, it remains a speculation and a hope. Utopia as the Omega Point shares in the eschatological mystery.

Let us leave our future prospects in abeyance, however, and focus on the past and present as best we can. Throughout this essay I have made a distinction between utopia as a social concept, an ideal for society at large, and utopia as a personal paradigm, a moral standard for the individual. I interpreted Plato's *Republic* as well as Thomas More's *Utopia* in the latter light, and I viewed the kingdom of God in its earthly dimension in a similar way. The personal and social aspects cannot be entirely separated, for the one inevitably involves the other, but a distinction nevertheless must be made. Our historical experience, I think, has taught us that to concentrate solely or even primarily on a utopian social goal can be disastrous. The ideal itself is transcendent. The kingdom of God is not of this world. The attempt to achieve it here and now only too readily lends itself to violent and despotic means. The best in this sense can be the enemy of the good, and the freedom essential to our human existence can in principle be denied and in fact be destroyed. But the social ideal can have a worldly extension; it can have the moral power to inspire and transform. It can be actualized on a personal scale, and through the individual it can have its effect on society and the world at large. Christ's parable of the mustard seed—the tiny seed that grows into a great shrub (Mk 4:30–32)—seems ingeniously appropriate. The passage from von Balthasar that I quoted at the outset should be understood in this way, I think. The yearning for perfection he speaks of is the sign of the Christian in his active life by virtue of his Christianity as well as his humanity.

This is certainly a subject that merits further discussion and exploration. I simply raise it at this point. I have, however, one last illustration of my theme: the recent encyclical of John Paul II concerned with the economic and social development of peoples.[24] It is a broad yet incisive critique of a world situation which prevents the "united cooperation of all for the common good of the human race," that is, which stands in the way of genuine human progress. Its analysis is surprisingly specific, and, as one might expect, the basic problems that hinder development are approached with a moral and religious perspective. One of the features that struck me most about the encyclical is the relationship it perceives between social or structural problems and personal moral acts. It stresses that social or structural evils "are rooted in personal sin, and thus always linked to the concrete acts of individuals who introduce these structures, consolidate them and make them difficult to remove." By the same token the encyclical seeks to guide Christian conduct and thus assist true development.

There are other parts of John Paul's encyclical that are pertinent to the topic we have been exploring. But a paragraph toward the end impressed me as particularly relevant, and with it I shall conclude this essay.

> The Church well knows that no temporal achievement is to be identified with the Kingdom of God, but that all such achievements simply reflect and in a sense anticipate the glory of the Kingdom, the Kingdom which we await at the end of history, when the Lord will come again. But that expectation can never be an excuse for the lack of concern for people in their concrete personal situations and in their social, national and international life, since the former is conditioned by the latter, especially today.

NOTES

1. *Convergences: To the Source of Christian Mystery,* trans. E. A. Nelson (San Francisco: Ignatius Press, 1983), p. 153. The passage bears out the comment in *The Encyclopedia of Religion,* s.v. "Utopia," that "utopia is fundamentally a given of religious consciousness."

2. Cf. *The City of God,* 14.28 and 15.1.

3. See Norman Cohn, *The Pursuit of the Millennium: Revolutionary Millenarians and Mystical Anarchists of the Middle Ages,* rev. ed. (New York: Oxford University Press, 1970).

4. Carl L. Becker, *The Heavenly City of the Eighteenth-Century Philosophers* (New Haven: Yale University Press, 1932); Robert Nisbet, *History of the Idea of Progress* (New York: Basic Books, 1980); Krishan Kumar, *Utopia and Anti-Utopia in Modern Times* (Oxford: Blackwell, 1987), Part I. See also Gertrude Himmelfarb's discussion of the theme in "History and the Idea of Progress," *The New History and the Old* (Cambridge: The Belknap Press of Harvard University Press, 1987).

5. P. 31.

6. *Works and Days* 109ff. Ovid in his *Metamorphoses,* Book I, also describes the Golden Age.

7. The proverb and Erasmus' discussion are found in *Adages: Ii1 to Iv100,* trans. Margaret Mann Phillips, Collected Works of Erasmus 31 (Toronto, Buffalo, and London: University of Toronto Press, 1982), pp. 15, 29–30. See also my essay "Erasmus' *Adagia* and More's *Utopia*" in *Moreana,* 100 (1989), 127–36.

8. Edd. Edward Surtz, s.j., and J. H. Hexter, The Yale Edition of the Complete Works of St. Thomas More 4 (New Haven and London: Yale University Press, 1965).

9. I name but a few to start the discussion: J. H. Hexter, *More's* UTOPIA: *The Biography of an Idea* (Princeton: Princeton University Press, 1952); Frank E. and Fritzie P. Manuel, *Utopian Thought in the Western World* (Cambridge: The Belknap Press of Harvard University Press, 1979), chap. 4; George M. Logan, *The Meaning of More's* UTOPIA (Princeton: Princeton University Press, 1983); Germán Arciniegas, *America in Europe: A History of the New World in Reverse,* trans. Gabriela Arciniegas and R. Victoria Arana (New York: Har-

court Brace Jovanovich, 1986), chap. 3; and Brendon Bradshaw, "More on Utopia," *The Historical Journal,* 24 (1981), 1–27.

10. See note 7 above.

11. From Erasmus' famous sketch of More, in a letter to Ulrich von Hutten, Ep. 999, in *Erasmi epistolae* IV, edd. P. S. Allen and H. M. Allen (Oxford: Clarendon Press, 1922), p. 21.

12. See Erasmus' *Paraclesis,* in *Christian Humanism and the Reformation: Selected Writings of Erasmus,* ed. John C. Olin, 3rd ed. (New York: Fordham University Press, 1987), p. 104; and my essay "The Pacifism of Erasmus," John C. Olin, *Six Essays on Erasmus* (New York: Fordham University Press, 1979), pp. 17–19.

13. Werner Jaeger's *Early Christianity and Greek Paideia* (Cambridge: The Belknap Press of Harvard University Press, 1969) springs to mind.

14. These words of Christ's are rendered in the original King James version as "the kingdom of God is within you."

15. *New Viewpoints on the Spanish Colonization of America,* trans. Joan Coyne (Philadelphia: University of Pennsylvania Press, 1943), p. 113. See also Arciniegas, *America in Europe,* pp. 68–70.

16. John Leddy Phelan, *The Millennial Kingdom of the Franciscans in the New World: A Study of the Writings of Gerónimo de Mendieta (1525–1604)* (Berkeley: University of California Press, 1956), chap. 7.

17. "Utopia and Geneva," in *Action and Conviction in Early Modern Europe,* edd. Theodore K. Rabb and Jerrold E. Siegel (Princeton: Princeton University Press, 1969), pp. 77–89.

18. See note 4 above.

19. *Heavenly City of the Eighteenth-Century Philosophers,* p. 139.

20. "The Second Coming," *The Collected Poems of W. B. Yeats* (New York: Macmillan, 1956), p. 185.

21. Commemorative edition (New York: New American Library, 1984), p. 258.

22. "History and the Idea of Progress," p. 155.

23. More continues his comment, adding " 'a situation which I do not expect for a great many years to come!' "

24. The encyclical is entitled *Sollicitudo rei socialis (The Social Concern of the Church)* and was issued February 19, 1988. The Catholic Truth Society, London, has published the English text.